Abstracts
of
HENRY COUNTY VIRGINIA

Deeds
(Books 1 *and* 2)

- 1776-1784 -

Compiled by:
Lela C. Adams

Southern Historical Press, Inc.
Greenville, South Carolina

Copyright 1975
By: Lela C. Adams

Copyright Transferred 1983
To: Southern Historical Press, Inc.

All rights reserved. No part of this publication may be reproduced, stored in a retrieval system, transmitted in any form, posted on to the web in any form or by any means without the prior written permission of the publisher.

Please direct all correspondence and orders to:

www.southernhistoricalpress.com
or
**SOUTHERN HISTORICAL PRESS, Inc.
PO BOX 1267
Greenville, SC   29601**
southernhistoricalpress@gmail.com

ISBN #0-89308-358-5

Printed in the United States of America

TABLE OF CONTENTS

INTRODUCTION iv

DEEDS, 17 FEBRUARY 1776 - 22 JULY 1784 . 1

SURVEYS, MARCH 1778 - JUNE 10, 1783. . .106

INDEX. 112

INTRODUCTION

In 1776, Patrick County was cut out of Pittsylvania County and was named for Patrick Henry. When first formed, Henry County embraced the whole of what is now Patrick County, and the greater portion of present Franklin County, Virginia.

These deeds include many bills of sale; trust deeds; powers of attorney; dower right releases; names of counties and states where the grantor has taken up residence or plans to reside; leases; damage suits; inquisitions into death; deeds of gifts; bonds and contracts.

DEDICATED TO

Shirley Brightwell Bassett

(Mrs. George W.)

Pages 1 and 2. 17 February 1776, Henry County, Virginia. JOHN HARDMAN and ELIZABETH his wife to THOMAS WILLINGHAM (WILLIHAM) both of the county of Henry, for the sum of sixty pounds does sell, convey, etc a tract or parcel of land containing 200 acres more or less, being part of a larger tract granted ____ HARDMAN, lottoins(?) patton baring the date 16 of ____ 1771, and bounded as follows: beginning with a red oak in URIAH HARDMAN'S line on Grassy Creek....(rest illegible)... Signed: JOHN HARDMAN, ELIZABETH HARDMAN. Signed in the presence of: SAMUEL LANIER.

Pages 2 and 3, Bond. JOHN ROWLAND, JOHN COX, ABRAM PENN, WILLIAM TUNSTALL of Henry County are bound unto ROBERT HAIRSTON, JAMES LYON, JONATHAN HANBY, ROBERT WOODS and PETER SAUNDERS, ESQ. Justice of the Peace for the said County. 17 day February 1777. The above obligation is such that whereas JOHN SALMON is constituted and appointed Sheriff of the said County. Signed: JOHN SALMONS, JOHN ROWLAND, JOHN COX, WILL. TUNSTALL, ABRAHAM PENN. Bond recorded at a Court held 17 February 1777. Teste: JOHN COX, C.H.C.

Pages 3 and 4. 8 February 1776. JOHN HARDMAN of Henry County to URIAH HARDMAN for the sum of thirty pounds, JOHN HARDMAN conveys, sells, etc to URIAH HARDMAN a certain tract of land containing by estimation 100 acres more or less, being a tract granted JOHN HARDMAN by letton(?) patent the 16 February 1761; bounded by a poplar on a small branch of the Marrowbone Creek to a white oak in the old line, etc; to a red oak on ELONAR TOLBORNS line at the head of a small branch, thence down the meadow of said creek to the beginning. Signed: JOHN (X) HARDMAN. Witness: SAMUEL LANIER, WILLIAM HARDMAN, THOMAS (X) WILLIHAM. Recorded 17 February 1777.

Pages 5 and 6. 17 February between THOMAS WILLIHAM of the county of Henry to THOMAS WILLIHAM, JR. of the same county in consideration of the sum of twenty pounds sells a certain tract containing by estimate 50 acres more or less, it being part of a tract of land granted said THOMAS WILLIHAM by bargain...(gives only tree boundries). Signed: THOMAS (X) WILLIHAM. Wit: SAMUEL LANIER. Recorded 17 February 1777 by JOHN COX.

Pages 6 and 7. 17 February 1777. THOMAS WILLIHAM of the county of Henry to JESSEY WILLIHAM of said county for the sum of twenty pounds conveys to him a certain tract containing by estimate 50 acres, it being part of a tract grant said THOMAS WILLIHAM by saill and bargain, beginning in a corner oak in THOMAS WILLIAM, JR. line, crossing a creek to a corner oak, etc. Signed: THOMAS (X) WILLIHAM, SR. Witness: SAMUEL LANIER. Recorded 17 February 1777.

Pages 8 and 9. 15 February 1777. ROBERT JONES of the county of Henry to MOSES RENTFRO of the county of Bedford, for the sum of forty pounds current money of Virginia conveys a certain tract of land containing 96 acres by patent bearing date at Williamburgh. Beginning in Henry County on the waters of the north fork of the Pigg River and bounded by a white oake, etc. Signed: ROBERT JONES.

Pages 9, 10, 11. 17 February 1777. ROBERT JONES of the County of Henry to DARBY RIAN of the said county aforesaid for the sum of thirty pounds current money of Virginia conveys and sells a parcel of land it being 127 acres by patent bearing date at Williamsburgh 15 June 1773, on the waters of Nicholases & Beards Creeks. Signed: ROBERT JONES.

Pages 11,12,13. 17 February 1777. ROBERT JONES of the county of Henry to GEORGE HAIRSTON of said county conveys for the sum of thirty five pounds a certain tract of land containing 228 acres in the county of Henry on the branch of Nicholases Creek. Signed: ROBERT JONES.

Pages 13, 14, 15. 17 February 1777. WILLIAM COOK of Henry County to PETER VARDEMAN of the same county for the sum of fifteen pounds, conveys land on both sides of Pigg River containing by estimate 20 acres, it being part of 210 acres whereon the said WILLIAM COOK now lives, it follows the river (Pigg) to the mouth of Hatchets Run. Signed: WILLIAM COOK. Wit: JOHN DICKENSON.

Pages 15, 16, 17. 17 February 1777. WILLIAM BLEVINS, SR. of the county of Henry to PHILLIP THOMAS of said county for the sum of one hundred and ten pounds sells to THOMAS 125 acres by estimate, it being patent granted WILLIAM BLEVINS bearing date March 10, 1756 in twenty nineth of the Reign. Beginning at a corner of RANDOLPH & Companys on the river (word river mentioned several times, but never named), thence to JOHN BLEVINS corner. Signed: WILLIAM (X) BLEVINS, AGNES (X) BLEVINS. AGNES BLEVINS wife of WILLIAM BLEVINS relinquishes her right of dower to the land.

Pages 18, 19, 20. 28 January 1777. RICHARD BREEDING of Henry County to JOHN STOCKTON of the county of Pittsylvania for the sum of fifty pounds sells 130 acres on both sides of the north fork of Mayo River, beginning on the north side of the River, crossing a branch of said river. Signed: RICHARD (X) BREEDING. Wit: ABRAHAM PENN, JOHN SOLMON, GEORGE HAIRSTON. FRANCES BREEDING, wife of RICHARD BREEDING, relinquishes her right of dower.

Pages 20, 21. 17 March 1777. JAMES POTEET of county of Henry to EDWARD PEDEGOYS of the same county for the sum of twenty five pounds conveys and sells to PEDEGOYS land on Elk Creek, to be taken off the upper end of the land said JAMES POTEET now lives on. Signed: JAMES POTEET.

Pages 22, 23, 24. 8 April 1775. RICHARD DOGGET of the county of Bedford to STEPHEN LEE of the county of Bedford for the sum of one hundred pounds, sells 160 acres more or less being on a branch of the Blackwater called Rich Run, beginning in RANDOLPH'S line. Signed: RICHARD DOGGET. Wit: NICHOLES ALEE, THOMAS MILLE, JOSEPH (X) ELLIS.

Pages 25, 26, 27. 10 February 1776. JOHN SIMS of the county of Henry to RALPH SHELTON of the same county for the sum of one hundred pounds, land on Green Creek on a branch of the South Mayo River, containing 119½ acres more or less. Signed: JOHN SIMS. Wit: ARCH. HUGHES, EDWARD (X) YOUNG, WILLIAM HAWKINS. SEPHIAH SIMS, wife of JOHN SIMS, relinquishes her right of dower.

Pages 27, 28. 8 February 1777. ABRAHAM WOMACK of the province of North Carolina in Orange County to JOHN KELLY of the county of Henry, state of Virginia, for the sum of thirty pounds sells said KELLY land in Henry County on the north side of Henry County, by estimate 326 acres, beginning at a branch to Elkins corner chestnut. Signed: ABRAHAM WOMACK. Wit: FRANCIS COX, NICHOLES PERKINS, BIMBEREY BENNET, FREDK. FITZGERALD.

Pages 29, 30. 21 April 1777. SAMUEL PATTERSON of the county of Henry and CRISLY(?), his wife to JAMES COWDEN of the same county for the sum of fifty pounds sell to said COWDEN 470 acres on the south side of Pigg River on a branch of Camp Creek.

Signed: SAMUEL PATTERSON, CECELY PATTERSON. Wit: JESSE HEARD, WILLIAM COWDON, JOHN JAMESON.

Pages 31, 32. 27 March 1777. PETER COPLAND of the county of Henry to WILLIAM BLEVINS of said county for the sum of sixty pounds, land it being on the waters of Bever Creek containing 120 acres beginning at a hickory of PATRICK COUTHS line crossing Little Beaver Creek, Great Beaver Creek. Signed: PETER COPLAND. Wit: WILLIAM BLEVINS, JR., GRYMES HAK.^m, JOHN BLEVINS.

Pages 32, 33, 34. 21 April 1777. JOHN FREDERICK MILLER of the county of Halifax to JAMES SHELTON of Henry County for the sum of three hundred pounds all that tract of land in Henry County on the north fork of Mayo River, beginning at the Bald Eagle Hill, running up said River on both sides plantation whereon JOHN CHILDRESS now lives containing 350 acres more or less it being part of a tract of 440 acres conveyed from THOMAS MANN RANDOLPH, Esq. to said JOHN FREDERICK MILLER by deed recorded in Pittsylvania County. Signed: JOHN FREDERICK MILLER. Wit: JOHN SALMON, DAVID LANIER, JOHN COX.

Pages 34, 35. 21 April 1777. JACOB COGER (KOGER) of Henry County to THOMAS STOCKTON of same for the sum of sixty pounds sells 94 acres on both sides of the north fork of the Mayo River. Signed: JACOB (X) COGAR.

Pages 35, 36, 37. 16 June 1777. JOSHUA MABRY and MARY his wife of Henry County to THOMAS JAMISON of the same county for the sum of ninety pounds sells land on the waters of Marrowbone Creek containing 134 acres, beginning at ABNER HARBOUR'S red oak corner...to the fork of Marrowbone Creek. Signed: JOSHUA MABRY, MARY MABRY. Wit: EDMD. LYNE, PETER SAUNDERS, JOHN COX. MARY MABRY, wife of JOSHUA relinquishes her right of dower.

Pages 38, 39, 40. 16 June 1777. AMBROS FLETCHER and HANNAH his wife of the county of Fincarsle (Fincastle ?) to JAMES DOAKE (DOAK) of the county of Surry and province of North Carolina. AMBROS FLETCHER for the sum of sixty three pounds sells to said DOAKE land in Henry County on Lovins Creek, a branch of the Ararat River, containing 166 acres more or less. Signed: AMB. FLETCHER, HANNAN (X) FLETCHER. HANNAH FLETCHER, wife of AMBROSE FLETCHER relinquishes her right of dower. Wit: PETER SAUNDERS, HUGH ARM-

STRONG, SAMUEL LYNE, JOHN COX, ARCHS. HUGHES.

Pages 41, 42. 8 June 1777. JOHN SALMON of the county of Henry to JOHN PACE of same for the sum of sixty five pounds sells to said PACE land in Henry County, it being 116 acres more or less appears by pattent granted unto CHARLES HARRIS. Beginning at an ash in EDMUND GRAYS & CO'S. line on Smith River to RANDOLPH & CO'S corner white oak. Signed: JOHN SALMON. Wit: JOHN COX, WILLIAM TUNSTALL, JOHN ALEXANDER, JR.

Pages 42, 43. 27 March 177_. RICHARD WOODING of the county of Halifax, executor of the will of JAMES MACKINTREE, deceased to HUMPHREY POSEY of the county of Pittsylvania for the sum of twenty-five pounds sells unto him land in Pittsylvania County it being 30 acres, which land was granted to DAVID HALY, letters patent bearing date 10 September 1755 and by him said HALY conveyed to JAMES MACKINTREE by deed recorded in Halifax County dated 21 January 1757. Land bounds description found in that deed. Signed: R. WOODING. Wit: JOHN COX, JOSEPH AKIN, JAMES SHELTON, SAMUEL MOSLEY, WILLIAMS ISAAC READ, H. MORGAN.

Pages 44, 45, 46. 18 July 1777. ROBERT BOLTON of county of Henry to LEVY SHOCKLEY of said county for the sum of twenty pounds sells land on the northwest side of Pigg River containing 43 acres. Signed: ROBERT BOULTON. Wit: CHALTON (X) SHOCKLEY, WILLIAM (X) ELLIS, ROBERT (X) BOLTON, JR.

Pages 46, 47, 48. 8 July 177_. HUGH INNES of the county of Henry to WILLIAM THARP for the sum of thirty pounds sells land on Otter Creek containing 150 acres. Signed: HUGH INNES.

Pages 48, 49, 50. 19 July 1777. WILLIAM MCDANIEL of Halifax County to CHRISTIAN RODE of Henry County for the sum of three hundred pounds land on both sides of Pigg River, beginning at a red oak on the north side of said River down it to the south side of River. Signed: WILLIAM McDANIEL. Wit: SPENCER SHELTON, WILLIAM McDANIEL, JR., CLEMENT McDANIEL.

Pages 50, 51. 12 May 1777. PETER COPLAND and ELIZABETH his wife to ROBERT DONALD of the county of Chesterfield for the sum of one hundred pounds sells to said DONALD 450 acres in the county of Henry which is on and crosses Daniels Creek. Signed: PETER COPLAND, ELIZABETH COPLAND. Wit: CHARLES

COPLAND, JOHN CUNNINGHAM, JR., JOHN ROLAND, JEREMEY JONES, THOMAS (X) JONES, JOHN MURCHEL.

Pages 52, 53. 21 July 1777. JOHN FREDERICK MILLER of the county of Halifax to JOHN GRESHAM of county of Henry for the sum of two hundred pounds, land containing 400 acres more or less in Henry County on both sides of Spoon Creek whereon said JOHN GRESHAM now lives. Signed: JOHN FREDERICK MILLER.

Pages 54, 55. 10 April 1777. SAMUEL BURNS of county of Henry to PHILLIP BROSHURS (BROSHEARS) for the sum of forty five pounds land in Henry County on the south side of Smith River containing by estimation 45 acres, beginning at FRANCIS GILLEY'S line on said river. Signed: SAMUEL BURNS, MARY ANN (X) BURNS. Wit: RUSSELL COX, TOLIVER COX, JOHN BOLLING.

Pages 56, 57. 14 January 1777. HENRY RICE of Wataga Settlement to THOMAS EDWARDS of the county of Pittsylvania for the sum of five hundred pounds a tract of land lying in said Pittsylvania County and being on the IRVIN (Smith) River and Home Creek, it being 200 acres more or less. Signed: HENRY RICE. Wit: WILLIAM EDWARDS, SR., SAMUEL SWEET, JAMES (X) EDWARDS.

Pages 58, 59. 10 February 1777. THOMAS BOULDIN of the County of Charlotte to MICHAEL WATSON of the county of Henry for the sum of thirty pounds sells to said WATSON 80 acres of land on the branches of the middle fork of Leatherwood Creek. Signed: THOMAS BOULDIN. Wit: ARCHD. SMITH, JOSEPH BOULDIN, DANIEL HANKINS, WILLIAM ALEXANDER, GEORGE TAYLOR.

Page 60. 18 August 1777. JAMES POTEET of the county of Henry to NATHAN HALL of the same county for the sum of one hundred eighty pounds sells all that divided tract of land on both sides of Elk Creek a branch of Irvin's (Smith) River, containing 300 acres more or less, it being part of a larger tract of 380 acres granted said JAMES POTEET by patent bearing date at Williamsburgh 27 August 1770, and adjoins the lower line of EDWARD PEDEGO. Signed: JAMES POTEET.

Pages 61, 62, 63. 17 March 1777. BENJAMIN STINNETT and USLEY his wife of the county of Henry to PETER HARRIS of the same county for the sum of seventy pounds sell to HARRIS 71 acres on the north side of Irvin (Smith) River, beginning at two red oaks in SAMUEL HUFF'S line, a white oak in THOMAS HOFF'S line. Signed: BENJAMIN STINNET (X). Wit: THOMAS HENDERSON, JOHN HENDERSON, JOHN KENDRICK.

Pages 63, 64, 65. 10 February 1777. THOMAS BOULDIN, SR. of the county of Charlotte to JOSEPH BOULDIN of the same county for the sum of two hundred pounds sells to said JOSEPH BOULDIN land in the county of Henry 765 acres on both sides of Mulberry Creek and joining Irvin (Smith) River, also joins lines of Randolph & Co. and Lomax & Co. Signed: THOMAS BOULDIN. Wit: DANIEL HANKINS, ARCHD. SMITH, WILLIAM ALEXANDER, GEORGE TAYLOR.

Pages 65, 66, 67. 20 June 1777. ARCHELUS HUGHES and JOHN WIMBISH of Henry County to JAMES DICKENSON of same county for the sum of seventy five pounds sells land containing 160 acres lying and being in Henry County on both sides of Spoon Creek it being land granted SAMUEL HARRIS patent bearing date 22 September 1766, adjoins MILLER'S line. Signed: ARCHS. HUGHES, JOHN WIMBISH. Wit: HENRY FRANCE, WILLIAM HAWKINS, BENJAMIN HAWKINS.

Pages 67, 68. 8 August 1777. THOMAS HARBOUR of the County of Pittsylvania to PHILLIP ANGLIN for the sum of two hundred and fifty pounds, a parcel of land containing 304 acres more or less on both sides of Fall Creek, beginning at an oak on the county line, to the north fork of the Mayo River. Signed: THOMAS HARBOUR. Wit: JOHN (X) JONSOAN, WILLIAM HAY, ABNER (X) HARBOUR, DAVID HARBOUR. SARAH HARBOUR, wife of THOMAS HARBOUR relinquishes her right of dower.

Pages 69, 70. 8 August 1770. THOMAS HARBOUR of the county of Pittsylvania to JOHN JOURNICAN of the county aforesaid for the sum of eight pounds sells to said JOURNECAN 50 acres more or less on both sides of Fall Creek. Signed: THOMAS HARBOUR. Wit: PHILLIP (X) ANGLIN, ABNER (X) HARBOUR, WILLIAM HAY, DAVID HARBOUR. SARAH HARBOUR, wife of THOMAS relinquishes right of dower.

Pages 70, 71. 10 September 1777. RALPH SHELTON, JR. to ROBERT BAKER of the province of North Carolina for the sum of one hundred forty pounds sells to said BAKER 119½ acres of land more or less on Green Creek in the county of Henry. Signed: RALPH SHELTON, JR. SUSANNA SHELTON, wife of RALPH SHELTON, JR. relinquishes her right of dower.

Pages 72, 73. 15 September 1777. SARAH HUTCHINSON of the county of Henry to JOEL ESTES for the sum of fifty nine pounds ten shillings sells to said ESTES land in Henry County on both sides of Grassey fork of Snow Creek containing 200 acres more or less, which tract was conveyed by SAMUEL PATTERSON to said SARAH HUTCHINSON by deed recorded in Pittsylvania County. Signed: SARAH (X) HUTCHINSON.

Page 73. 20 October 1777. ALLEN RIDLEY YOUNG of the county of Henry to JOEL ADKINSON of the same county for the sum of fifteen pounds conveys to said ADKINSON 70 acres of land on Snow Creek. Signed: ALLEN RIDLEY YOUNG.

Pages 74, 75. 4 May 1777. PETER COPLAND of county of Henry to THOMAS COOPER of the same county for the sum of seventy seven pounds ten shillings conveys land on Beaver Creek it being 200 acres more or less, lines: JOSEPH COOPER, AMBROSE JONES. Signed: PETER COPLAND. Wit: TIMOTHY STAMP, JAMES ANTHONY, GEORGE ELLOTT, THOMAS GARNER, CHARLES COPLAND.

Pages 75, 76, 77. 13 October 1777. PETER COPLAND of the county of Henry to ANTHONY BITTING of the state of Maryland for the sum of two hundred pounds sells to said BITTING land in Henry County containing 280 acres more or less...lines: Blevin's, Couth's, Penn's and Beaver Creek. Signed: PETER COPLAND. Wit: SALLY COPLAND, IGNATIOUS SIMS, EDWARD (X) POLLY.

Pages 77, 78. 20 October 1777. ROBERT BOULTON of Henry County to THOMAS BOULTON of the same for the sum of one hundred thirty pounds sells to said THOMAS BOULTON 260 acres more or less in Henry County on both sides of Pigg River...lines: ROBERT POWELL and JOHN ELLIS. Signed: ROBERT BOULTON.

Pages 78, 79. 16 October 1777. PETER COPLAND of the county of Henry to THOMAS COOPER, JR. of said county for the sum of one hundred seventy two pounds and ten shillings conveys, sells land on the waters of Beaver Creek, it being 330 acres more or less, adjoining the land of JOSEPH COOPER. Signed: PETER COPLAND.

Pages 79, 80. 20 October 1777. WILLIAM BLEVINS of Henry County to JOHN COOPER of same county for the sum of eighty pounds conveys land on the waters of Beaver Creek containing 120 acres, lines:

PATRICK COULLS (?), Little Beaver Creek. Signed: WILLIAM (X) BLEVINS.

Pages 81, 82. 19 September 1777. THOMAS MANN RANDOLPH of the county of Goochland to JOSIAS CARTER of Pittsylvania county for the sum of two hundred five pounds land in Henry County containing 212 acres, beginning below the mouth of Read Creek upon the Irvin (Smith) River. Signed: THOMAS M. RANDOLPH. Wit: WILLIAM RYAN, JOSEPH (X) BAKER, THOMAS (X) DOOLY, JOSEPH WALKER.

Pages 82, 83. 20 May 1777. PETER COPLAND of the county of Pittsylvania to THOMAS GARDINER of the same county for the sum of ten pounds conveys to said GARDINER 72 acres more or less on the ___ Creek in Pittsylvania County. Signed: PETER COPLAND. Wit: DAVID MATLOCK, JAMES HODGILL, THOMAS COOPER, SR., TIMOTHY STAMPS, JAMES ANTHONY, GEORGE ELLIOTT.

Pages 83, 84, 85. 14 May 1777. JAMES ANTHONY of the county of Henry to THOMAS COOPER, JR. of the same for the sum of thirty pounds conveys 150 acres more or less in the county of Henry adjoining the lands of JOSEPH COOPER. Signed: JAMES ANTHONY.

Page 85. 20 October 1777. ROBERT BOULTON of county of Henry to EUSIBUS HUBBARD of same county for the sum of seventy five pounds conveys to him, 350 acres on Snow Creek. Signed: ROBERT BOULTON.

Page 86. Relinquish right of dower, 16 October 1777. To: NATHANIEL TERRY, WILLIAM TERRY, JAMES BATES and JOHN COLEMAN, Esqs., Justices of the Peace of Halifax County; whereas, WILLIAM McDANIEL has conveyed land unto CHRISTIAN RODE in Henry County, 300 acres, and whereas the wife of the said MC DANIEL cannot conveniently travel to and from said county of Henry, knowing your faithful and provident circumstances would examine the wife of said McDANIEL, ANN McDANIEL to see if she reliquishes her right of dower to this transaction, etc. . . .Halifax County... Justices JAMES BATES and WILLIAM TERRY did examine ANN, wife of said WILLIAM MCDANIEL and she willingly relinquishes her right of dower in regards to this deed to CHRISTIAN RHODES.

Page 87. 16 December 1777. Relinquish right of dower. To: Justices of Henry County: ROBERT CHANDLER conveyed unto STEPHEN MUIRS 220 acres of land in Henry County and the wife of said ROBERT CHANDLER, PERTHENEY CHANDLER, cannot conveniently travel to court etc....We have examined said PERTHENY CHANDLER, wife of ROBERT CHANDLER, and she willingly relinquishes her right of dower to the 220 acres of land conveyed unto STEPHEN MIERS. Signed: GEORGE WALLER, THOMAS HAMILTON.

Pages 88, 89, 90. 23 October 1777. JOHN HEARD and SUSANAH his wife of the county of Henry to SPENCER CLACK of the county of Loudon for the sum of one hundred forty five pounds sell land in Henry County on both sides of Crabtree fork of Snow Creek containing 150 acres, it being part of a tract of 200 acres granted by patent to OBEDIAH WOODSON bearing date 10 September 1755 and by him conveyed to NICKOLAS PERKINS LEVINS and by said LEVINS the said tract of 150 acres to JOHN HEARD. Signed: JOHN HEARD, SUSANNA HEARD. Wit: HUGH INNES, BENJAMIN COOK.

Pages 90, 91. 22 October 1777. ...Same Deed as appears on pages 88-90, JOHN HEARD and wife SUSANAH to SPENCER CLACK...150 acres on Snow Creek.

Pages 91, 92. 16 February 1778. JAMES DOKE of the county of Surry and province of North Carolina to HUGH ARMSTRONG of the county of Henry state of Virginia, for the sum of six hundred pounds sells land, etc in Henry County on both sides Lovins Creek, a branch of the Ararat River containing 160 acres. Signed: JAMES DOOKE.

Page 93. 15 December 1777. In the 2nd year of American Independence, GEORGE DEATHERAGE of Surry County, North Carolina to WILLIAM HOLBART (HOLBERS) of same county, land in Henry County, Virginia for the sum of two hundred pounds land on both sides of Russell's Creek a branch of the Mayo River containing 170 acres adjoining lines of JOHN PARR and JOHN HUNTER. Signed: GEORGE DEATHERAGE. Wit: JAMES LYON, JOHN DUNCAN, JOSEPH CLOUD, JAMES GATES, JOHN PARR.

Pages 94, 95. 6 October 1777. SHEM COOK of Henry County to WILLIAM HUNTER of same for the sum of five hundred pounds conveys land on Buham Town Creek of Smith River by estimate 303 acres, it being land granted SHEM COOK by patent bearing date 16 February 1771, adjoining WILLIAM STANLEY. Signed: SHEM COOK. Wit: HUGH INNES, EDGECOMB G. WILLIAMS, WILLIAM JAMESON.

Pages 95, 96, 97. 5 January 1778. PETER COPLAND of Henry County and his wife ELIZABETH to WILLIAM BLACK of the county of Chesterfield for the sum of one thousand eight hundred pounds conveys land in Henry County by estimate to contain 10,052 acres on the north fork of the Dan River. Signed: PETER COPLAND, ELIZABETH COPLAND.

Pages 97, 98, 99. 6 January 1778. PETER COPLAND and ELIZABETH his wife of Henry County to WILLIAM BLACK of the county of Chesterfield for the sum of three hundred sixty pounds conveys 3,350 acres of land located and being in Henry County...one tract 1,550 acres adjoining Black's land on Dan River; another tract of 1,000 acres adjoining his own land and then one tract of 800 acres. Signed: PETER COPLAND, ELIZABETH COPLAND.

Page 99. 19 January 1778. JOSEPH MAYBERY (MABRY) and MARY his wife of Henry County to SPENCER CLACK of same for the sum of one hundred fifty pounds conveys 250 acres land, it being part of a tract formerly granted OBEDIAH WOODSON 10 September 1755, adjoining lines of : JOHN HEARD, WALKER on Crabtree Fork of Snow Creek. Signed: JOSEPH MABRY, SUSANNA (?) MABRY. Wit: JOHN HEARD, SUSANNAH HEARD (X), JAMES (X) CARGILL.

Page 100. 29 December 1778. THOMAS COOPER of county of Henry to PETER COPLAND for the sum of six pounds, 4 acres of land adjoining COPLAND'S own land. Signed: THOMAS COOPER. Wit: GEORGE ELLIOTT, JAMES ANTHONY, TIMOTHY STAMPS, THOMAS GARNER, CHARLES COPLAND, JAMES COOPER, AMBROSE JONES.

Pages 101, 102. 16 February 1778. WILLIAM STEWART of Henry County to JOHN WYATT for the sum of thirty five pounds sells land on Rockey Branch of Leatherwood Creek...lines: Rock Spring Branch. Containing 150 acres more or less. Signed: WILLIAM (X) STEWART. . .RACHEL, wife of WILLIAM STEWART relinquishes her right of dower.

Pages 102, 103. 6 November 1777. SALLY COPLAND of the county of Henry to PETER COPLAND for the sum of ten pounds conveys, sells, etc. to the said PETER COPLAND 7,675 acres more or less on the Dan River. Signed: SALLY COPLAND. Wit: AMBROSE JONES, WINNEY (X) JONES, CHARLES COPLAND.

Page 104. 27 December 1777. PETER COPLAND of the

county of Henry to HENRY DUNLAP of the same
county for the sum of sixty pounds conveys, sells,
153 acres on Reedy Creek. Signed: PETER COPLAND.

Pages 105, 106. 14 January 1778. JOHN BOLLING and
REBACAH his wife of Henry County to
JACOB STALLING of Montgomery County state of Maryland
for the sum of seventy pounds sell 90 acres more or
less on the south side of Smith River. Signed: JOHN
BOLLING, REBECAH BOLLING. Wit: JOHN COX, R. FARGUSON,
MARY COX, JAMES (X) MOLLEY.

Pages 106, 107. 14 October 1777. THOMAS WILLIHAM,
SR. and MARY his wife of the county
of Henry to ANDREW RAY of the same for the sum of
eighty pounds sells 100 acres more or less, it being
part of a larger tract granted said WILLIHAM by bargain (recorded in Henry County) adjoining URIAH HARD-
MAN, THOMAS WILLIHAM, JR. and Grassy Creek. Signed:
THOMAS WILLIHAM. Wit: SAMUEL LANIER, DAVID LANIER,
JOHN WILLINGHAM, JESSEY WILLINGHAM.

Pages 108, 109. 16 March 1778. URIAH HARDMAN and
FANEY his wife of the county of Henry
to JESSEY WILLINGHAM for the sum of one hundred pounds
sell 100 acres on a small branch on Marrowbone Creek
adjoins ELONER TALBORN'S line. Signed: URIAH HARDMAN,
FANEY HARDMAN. Wit: SAMUEL LANIER, JOSEPH EAST,
CHARLES HARDMAN.

Pages 109, 110. 16 March 1778. JESSEY WILLINGHAM
and his wife FRANCES to JOHN MANNUN
of Henry County for the sum of thirty three pounds
sell 50 acres on a creek not named adjoining ROBERT-
SON. Signed: JESSE WILLINGHAM, FANNEY WILLINGHAM.

Pages 110, 111. 24 October 1777. BENJAMIN HICKS and
MARTHA his wife of Brunswick County
to GEORGE BOLING of Henry County for the sum of five
pounds sells 2 acres more or less on the north side
of Marrowbone Creek. Signed: BENJAMIN HICKS. Wit:
SAMUEL LANIER, DAVID LANIER, JOHN KING.

Pages 111, 112, 113. 21 November 1777. ARCHIBALD
ROBERTSON of Henry County to
JOSEPH ANTHONY of the county of Bedford for the sum
of four hundred pounds five shillings sells a certain
parcel of land which the said ROBERTSON bought of
BURDETT ERSKRIDGE in Henry County on Marrowbone Creek
containing 345 acres on a branch of Marrowbone Creek.
Signed: ARCHIBALD ROBERTSON. Wit: DAVID LANIER,

ARTHUR ROBERTSON, JOHN RAMY, ALEXANDER MCKEEN.

Pages 113, 114. 8 December 1777. THOMAS WILLINGHAM, JR. of county of Henry to ARCHIBALD ROBERTSON for the sum of thirty eight pounds five shillings sells 50 acres more or less on Grassey Creek and the branches thereof; Lines: ANDREW REA, JESSE WILLINGHAM, THOMAS WILLINGHAM, JR. Signed: THOMAS WILLINGHAM. Wit: SAMUEL LANIER, JESSE WILLINGHAM, ANDREW REA, ARTHUR ROBERTSON.

Pages 114, 115, 116. 12 January 1778. JAMES COX, SR. of the county of Pittsylvania to JAMES COX, JR. of the county of Henry for the sum of ten pounds sells 267 acres more or less in the county of Pittsylvania on the waters of Leatherwood Creek adjoins Lomax & Co. and Youngton's lines. Signed: JAMES COX.

Pages 116, 117. 13 December 1777. ROBERT HOOKER of the county of Henry to WILLIAM LOVELL of the county of Pittsylvania for the sum of one hundred ten pounds sells 150 acres of land, it being the residue of a patent obtained from the Secretary's Office for 400 acres, reference being to said patent more fully appear. Signed: ROBERT (X) HOOKER. Wit: WILLIAM TUNSTALL, SAMUEL TARRANT, JONATHAN (X) SWANN, JOSEPH GRAVELY.

Pages 117, 118. 15 March 1778. HENRY LYNE and EDMUND LYNE of Henry County to WILLIAM TACKETT of same county, the said HENRY & EDMUND LYNE by virtue of a deed of trust to them made by THOMAS BULLOCK of Pittsylvania County for payment of a certain sum of money both for and in consideration of twenty five pounds the LYNES sell to TACKETT a parcel of land in Henry County on Smith River being the place whereon the said TACKETT now lives containing 77 acres on the east side of Smith River along the county line. Signed: HENRY LYNE, EDMUND LYNE.

Pages 118, 119. 18 April 1778. ROBERT JONES, JR. of Henry County to ELIJAH JONES for the sum of twenty pounds sells 108 acres it being part of a tract of land being on both sides of the North Fork of Pig River by patent bearing date at Williamsburgh 26 September 1760, reference there being made will more fully appear. Joins WALTER MATHEWS. Signed: ROBERT JONES, JR. Wit: WILLIAM MAVITY, JOHN BANKS, DARBY RYAN.

Pages 119, 120. 18 April 1778. ROBERT JONES, JR. of the county of Henry to DAVID JONES for the sum of twenty pounds sells a parcel of land containing 112 acres being a part of a larger tract on both sides of Pig River as described in the above deed. Signed: ROBERT JONES, JR. Wit: WILLIAM MAVITY, JOHN BANKS, DARBY RYAN.

Page 121. 17 November 1777. THOMAS POTTER of Henry County to ELISHA WALKER of Pittsylvania County for the sum of twenty five pounds sells 100 acres more or less on the south side of Pigg River in Henry County, joins JENKIN'S line, land lying opposite to Tacks Creek. Signed: THOMAS POTTER.

Pages 121, 122, 123. 4 March 1778. ISSAAC JONES of the county of Henry to PETER YOUNG of the same for the sum of thirty seven pounds ten shillings conveys 205 acres of land, being part of a tract on which the said JONES now lives, containing in the whole 400 acres by patent at Williamburgh, the land being on both sides of Pigg River. Signed: ISAAC JONES, RACHEL JONES, his wife.

Pages 123, 124. 22 November 1777. SOLOMAN DAVIS of the county of Henry to JOHN GRIMMIT for the sum of seventeen pounds ten shillings sells land containing 100 acres on a branch on HARDAINS & HALLS line, FREDERICK RIVES line, ELECTIOUS HARDAINS line. Signed: SOLOMON DAVIS. Wit: FREDERICK RIVES, ELECTIOUS HARDAIN, THOMAS POTTER.

Pages 124, 125. 18 April 1778. WILLIAM GRAVES, SR. of the county of Henry to WILLIAM GRAVES, JR. for the sum of ten pounds conveys 100 acres of land more or less in the county of Henry; lines: COCKERHAM'S and NATHANIEL LAW'S. Signed: WILLIAM GRAVES.

Pages 125, 126. 20 April 1778. WILLIAM COOK of Henry County, Virginia to JOHN BOHANNON of the same county for the sum of forty pounds conveys 50 acres of land on both sides of Pig River. Signed: WILLIAM COOK.

Pages 126, 127. 28 August 1777. Bond of Indenture. Witness that GEORGE COX doth bind his three children, GEORGE COX, JAMES COX and MARY COX unto WILLIAM EDWARDS and his wife of the county of Henry until said children shall be of age. Being at the age of 9 years 3 months GEORGE and JAMES and MARY

at the age of 3 years 4 months doth put the said
children to WILLIAM EDWARDS and wife to be brought up
in a regular manner to serve him and her from the day
of the date hereof until the said children shall be
of age, all which time the said GEORGE, MARY and JAMES
COX will faithfully serve their master and mistress.
They will keep all lawful commandments everywhere and
gladly obey. They shall do no damage to the said
master or mistress, they shall not waste their said
masters or mistress goods nor lend them unlawfully to
any. They shall not commit fornication nor contract
matrimony during the said term they shall not absent
themselves day or night form said master or mistress,
but in all things behave themselves faithfully, and
the said master and mistress shall provide for them
sufficient meat, drink, washing, lodging and apparel
and other necessarys among the said term likewise to
learn them to read the old and new Testament and give
them a suit of common apparel at the end of the said
term. Signed: GEORGE (X) COX, WILLIAM EDWARDS, ANN
(X) EDWARDS.

Pages 127, 128. 21 October 1777. PETER COPLAND of
the county of Henry to GEORGE HAMIL-
TON of Prince George County in Maryland for the sum
of two hundred twenty five pounds conveys land on the
waters of Beaver Creek containing 680 acres more or
less beginning at ANTHONY BITTINGS corner, ABRAM PENN'S
line, crossing Little Beaver Creek, JOHN COOPER'S
line. Signed: PETER COPLAND. Wit: RICHARD COPLAND,
CHARLES COPLAND, SALLY COPLAND, EDMUND LYNE, JAMES
LYON, WILLIAM TUNSTALL.

Pages 128, 129. 14 April 1778. PETER COPLAND of the
county of Henry to AMOS RICHARDSON
of the same for the sum of fifty pounds paid by JOHN
MINTER, land containing 220 acres more or less on
Reedy Creek. Signed: PETER COPLAND.

Page 130. Relinquish right of dower. To FREDERICK
RIVES & JESSE HEARD, Esqs or any two Justices of Henry County, Virginia, whereas JOSEPH MABRY
has conveyed unto SPENCER CLACK in Henry County land
containing 250 acres and whereas MARY, said wife of
JOSEPH MABRY cannot conveniently travel to the Courthouse she does hereby relinquish her right of dower
to the above land. Signed: JOHN COX.

Page 131. Bond. Bond of JOHN SALMON with WILLIAM
TUNSTALL, GEORGE HAIRSTON, JOHN ROWLAND,
JOHN BLAGG and JOHN COX as his bondsmen for said JOHN

SALMON to be appointed to the office of Sheriff.

Pages 131, 132. Bond. JOHN SALMON, WILLIAM TUNSTALL, GEORGE HAIRSTON, JOHN ROWLAND, JOHN BLAGG and JOHN COX of the county of Henry are bound unto the Commonwealth of Virginia in the penal sum of thirty six thousand one hundred and twenty pounds of tobacco to which payment will and truly be made the Treasurer for the time being we bind ourselves firmly by these presents. The condition of the above obligation is such that if the above bound JOHN SALMON, Sheriff, will collect and receive of and from each Tithable person 14# tobacco that is laid on each tithable by an Act of the Assembly for raising a publick levey and duly account.

Pages 132, 133. 30 April 1778. JAMES SHELTON of the county of Henry to JOSIAH SMITH of the same for the sum of two hundred sixteen pounds sells land on the branches of Horsepasture Creek being part of a tract which said SHELTON purchased of THOMAS MAN RANDOLPH, it being two hundred sixteen acres (216 acres). Signed: JAMES SHELTON, PHILIPHIAH SHELTON, his wife. Wit: WILLIAM SHELTON, LOT IVIE, JOSEPH CAMRON.

Pages 133, 134. 26 April 1778. GIDEON RUCKER of the county of Henry to DANIEL RICHARDSON of the same for the sum of one hundred pounds sells 100 acres being on Crabtree fork of Snow Creek adjoining lines of SPENCER CLACK and AMOS RICHARDSON. Signed: GIDEON RUCKER. Wit: AARON MACKENZIE, JAMES COOK, JOSHUA WILLINGHAM, WILLIAM RYAN.

Pages 134, 135. 18 May 1778. Apprenticeship. LEWIS THOMSON, son of MARY THOMSON, late of Henry County doth put himself voluntarily apprentice to CHRISTAIN ROADS a potter of Henry County for four years from 27 January last. He doth promise that he shall not play dice or cards or any unlawful game, nor hant alehouses nor taverns nor playhouses, but in all things behave himself... Signed: LEWIS THOMPSON, CHRISTIAN ROADS. Wit: JOHN DICKENSON.

Pages 135, 136. 21 April 1778. ELIZABETH COPLAND wife of PETER COPLAND doth hereby relinquish right of dower in a deed of PETER COPLAND to GEORGE HAMILTON for 608 acres.

Page 137. Relinquish right of dower. ELIZABETH COPLAND wife of PETER COPLAND relinquishes her right of dower to 450 acres conveyed by PETER COPLAND to ROBERT DONALD of Chesterfield County.

Pages 137, 138. 12 May 1778. JACOB COX of the county of Henry to DANIEL CARLIN of the same for the sum of ninety pounds conveys 236 acres of land on both sides of Stewards Creek of the Ararat River. This being part of a tract granted HENRY LANSFORD by patent dated 3 August 1771. Signed: JACOB COX. Wit: JONATHAN HANBY, ELIPHAZ SHELTON, GEORGE CARTER.

Pages 138, 139. 10 May 1778. JOHN DANIEL, SR. of the county of Henry to ALEXANDER HUNTER for the sum of two hundred fifty pounds land on both sides of the South Mayo River, it being the land granted JONATHAN HANBY by patent bearing date 16 March 1771, mentions the foot of a mountain (not named). Signed: JOHN (X) DANIEL. Wit: GEORGE CARTER, ELIPHAZ SHELTON, JONATHAN HANBY.

Page 140. December 1775. Then received of DILLION BLEVINS full satisfaction for all debts and contracts between us from the day of creation of the world to this day. The said BLEVINS paying to JOHN SALMON his commission for selling to negros, I say received. Signed: THOMAS STOAKES. . . .At a Court held 16 day of June 1778 on the motion of DILLION BLEVINS the with receipt was ordered to be recorded. Signed: JOHN COX, Clerk Henry Co.

Pages 140, 141. 22 November 1777. WILLIAM STEGALL of Halifax County to WILLIAM GRAVES of Henry County for the sum of one hundred sixty pounds sells a tract by estimate 500 acres more or less on the south side of Pigg River, beginning with a Juniper tree on WILLIAM HAYNES line to a black oak on ABNER COCKARHAM'S line. Signed: WILLIAM (X) STEGALL. Wit: WILLIAM WITCHER, SAMUEL BOLLING, DAVID WILLIS, THOMAS BOULTON, BENJAMIN (X) PATTON, JOHN (X) LAW.

Pages 141, 142, 143. 27 May 1778. RICHARD WITTON of the County of Mecklinburg and parish of St. James to JOHN LAW of the county of Henry, planter, for the sum of one hundred sixty pounds a certain parcel of land by estimate 2,204 acres more or less in Henry County. Being part of a patent granted WITTON for 5,316 acres dated 26 July 1765, lying on the waters of Simmon's Creek. Mentions: Jack's Mountain, JAMES COWDON'S outside line of survey of 350 acres sold him. Signed: RICHARD WITTON.

Wit: WILLIAM GRAVES, JOHN LAW, JR., JESSE LAW, HENRY LAW.

Pages 143, 144. 28 February 1778. NATHAN HALL of the county of Henry to WILLIAM EAST of said county for the sum of fifty pounds sells a parcel of land containing 100 acres more or less on Little Marrowbone Creek beginning at a poplar upon EDMOND GRAY'S order line with a straight course north to POOLS branch commonly called BLEVINS line, all the land under the mountain on both sides of the said creek out of said EDMUND GRAY'S order line. Signed: NATHAN HALL. Wit: JOHN PAYNE, JOSIAH PAYNE, REUBEN PAYNE, THOMAS LEAKE.

Pages 144, 145. 20 July 1778. WILLIAM HUNTER to ARTHUR EDWARDS both of the Parish of Camden and county of Henry, colony of Virginia. For the sum of four hundred pounds conveys land on the waters of Snow Creek and Beaver Creek beginning at a white oak in GEORGE WALKER'S line, containing 500 acres more or less. Signed: WILLIAM HUNTER. CHAIRTY HUNTER, wife of WILLIAM HUNTER relinquishes her right of dower to the above land.

Page 146. 18 January 1778. WILLIAM WEBB of the county of Henry to ROBERT BOULTON of the same for the sum of four shillings sells 1 acre of land more or less in Henry County on the north side of Pigg River, beginning at ROBERT BOULTON'S corner mahaggony tree. Signed: WILLIAM (X) WEBB. Wit: JAMES (X) BOULTON, ROBERT (X) BOULTON, ANN (X) BOULTON, MAN (X) BOULTON.

Pages 147, 148. 15 August 1777. NATHANIEL LAW of Henry County to NATHAN BARNETT for the sum of twenty pounds conveys 100 acres more or less on the east side of Owen's Creek, crossing the creek to ANDERSON'S line. Signed: NATHANIEL (X) LAW and his wife. Wit: ROBERT (X) BOULTON, MARY (X) BOULTON, ANN (X) BOULTON.

Pages 148, 149. 18 January 1778. WILLIAM WEBB of Henry County to WILLIAM HAMMON of Pittsylvania County for the sum of thirty five pounds sells land 100 acres, more or less, on the north side of Pigg River, oak in ROBERT BOULTON'S line, mahaggany tree to WILLIAM HAYNES' corner poplar. Signed: WILLIAM (X) WEBB. Wit: JAMES (X) BOULTON, ROBERT (X) BOULTON, MARY (X) BOULTON.

Page 149, 150. 17 August 1778. MICHAEL MADOX of Henry County to HUGH INNES of same for the sum of seventy five pounds conveys land on the waters of Chestnut Creek, 108 acres beginning at a red oak on a spur of the Chestnut Mountain. Signed: MICHAEL (X) MADOX. Wit: ABRAHAM PENN, JOHN HEARD, JAC. MAOROW. . . .17 August 1778 - HANNAH, wife of MICHAEL MADOX relinquishes her right of dower to the above land.

Pages 150, 151. 17 August 1778. ELISHA EASTES, SR. of the county of Henry to ELISHA EASTES, JR. of same for one hundred pounds conveys land on the waters of Goard Creek it being 100 acres more or less beginning at ROBERT BOOLMANS (BOULTON ?) corner thence along the Court House Road to JEFFERSON'S line. Signed: ELISHA (X) ESTES. FRANCES ESTES, wife of ELISHA ESTES relinquishes her right of dower to the above land.

Pages 151, 152. Relinquish right of dower. ELIZABETH COPLAND, wife of PETER COPLAND relinquishes her right of dower to sale of land to THOMAS COOPER containing 300 acres.

Pages 152, 153. Same as above. . .ELIZABETH COPLAND relinquishes her right of dower in transaction to THOMAS COOPER of 320 acres.

Pages 153, 154. 25 April 1778. ELIZABETH COPLAND wife of PETER COPLAND relinquishes her right of dower to 200 acres conveyed unto THOMAS COOPER.

Pages 154, 155, 156. 11 November in the XIII year of the Reighn of our Soverign Lord King George Third in the year of our Christ 1773 between HENRY RICE of Pittsylvania County of the one part and ARCHELAUS HUGHES and JOHN WIMBISH of the other part of the same, for the sum of twenty five pounds land on the North Fork of the Mayo River containing 180 acres more or less which was granted said RICE by patent bearing date 16 March 1771. Signed: HENRY RICE. Wit: FREDERICK FULKERSON, LEO. VANDEGREFT, HENRY FRANCE. . .Entered into record 20 July 1778.

Page 156. Relinquish right of dower. OBEDIAH HUDSON sold to WILLIAM ROBERT HUDSON of Henry County 175 acres of and RHODA the wife of said OBEDIAH HUDSON doth hereby relinquish her right of dower.

Pages 157, 158. 4 June 1778. STEPHEN MARES and JANE his wife of Henry County to ALEXANDER JOYCE for the sum of two hundred twenty five pounds sells 250 acres more or less on the branches of Marrowbone Creek...mentions MCKEENS line. Signed: STEPHEN MARIS, JEAN MARIS.

Pages 159, 160. 21 September 1778. CHARLES FINCH and JOYCE his wife of Henry County to GEORGE HAIRSTON sell and convey for the sum of fifty pounds land containing by patent 180 acres more or less on the north side of Irvin (Smith) River, crossing Mill Creek, joining RANDOLPHS, HARMON & KINGS lines. Signed: CHARLES FINCH, JOYCE (X) FINCH.

Pages 160, 161, 162. 15 September 1778. PETER COPLAND and ELIZABETH his wife of Henry County to WILLIAM BLACK of the county of Chesterfield for the sum of one thousand six hundred pounds convey and sell a tract of land containing 7,675 acres more or less on the Dan River...crosses the north fork of the Dan River. Signed: PETER COPLAND, ELIZABETH COPLAND.

Pages 162, 163. 21 September 1778. JOHN SIMMONS and NANCY his wife to IGNATIOUS SIMMS of Henry County for the sum of seventy five pounds convey 177 acres, by estimate, on the branches of Beaver Creek. Signed: JOHN SIMMONS, NANCY SIMMONS.

Pages 163, 164. 21 September 1778. PETER COPLAND of Henry County to JOHN GOOD of the same county for the sum of thirty eight pounds conveys land on little Reedy Creek containing by estimate 160 acres more or less, beginning at WILLIAM HEARD'S corner pointer. Signed: PETER COPLAND.

Page 165. 21 September 1778. PETER COPLAND of the county of Henry to WILLIAM HEARD for the sum of forty pounds on little Ready Creek land being 140 acres more or less...mentions pointer in ROBERTS line. Signed: PETER COPLAND.

Pages 166, 167. 21 July 1778. JOSIAH CARTER of Henry County to BAYNES CARTER of same county for the sum of one hundred three pounds and four shillings conveys and sells a tract or parcel of land situated in said county on Reedy Creek 89½ acres beginning at a white oak in RANDOLPH'S old order line crossing little Reedy Creek, crosses Reed Creek to the mouth of said creek on Smith River.

Signed: JOSIAH CARTER. Wit: JOHN DICKERSON, JOHN (X) CROUCH, JOHN PURSELL. . .NANCY CARTER, wife of JOSIAH CARTER relinquishes her right of dower to the above transaction.

Pages 167, 168. 21 September 1778. FRANCES COX of the county of Henry to JOSEPH GRAVELY for the sum of ten shillings conveys a certain parcel of land situated in Henry County on a branch of Leatherwood Creek beginning at WILLIAM LOVELL'S corner oak, containing by estimate 200 acres more or less. Signed: FRANCIS COX.

Pages 168, 169. 21 August 1778. HENRY DUNLAP of the county of Henry to MICHAEL DYLINGHAM of county aforesaid for the sum of three hundred pounds conveys a tract on Reedy Creek containing 153 acres, it being the land on which HENRY DUNLAP now lives. Signed: HENRY (X) DUNLAP.

Pages 169, 170. Relinquish right of dower. ELIZABETH COPLAND wife of PETER COPLAND relinquishes her right of dower to two tracts of land said PETER COPLAND conveyed unto JOSEPH COOPER containing 112 acres and 258 acres. Signed: ABRAHAM PENN, GEORGE WALLER, Justices of Henry County, Va.

Pages 170, 171. 19 October 1778. WILLIAM MULLINGS of the county of Henry to WILLIAM MULLINGS, JR. of the same county for the sum of one hundred pounds conveys 290 acres on the east fork of Town Creek...crosses north fork. Signed: WILLIAM MULLINS. . .ELIZABETH MULLINS, wife of WILLIAM MULLINS, relinquishes her right of dower to the above transaction.

Page 172. 29 September 1778. THOMAS JONES of county of Henry to WILLIAM MENIFEE, JR. of aforesaid county for the sum of four hundred pounds conveys land on both sides of Pigg River...west crossing a Bold Branch. Signed: THOMAS JONES, SR. Wit: PETER SAUNDERS, CALEB TATE, THOMAS HALE. . .MARY JONES, wife of THOMAS JONES relinquishes right of dower to the above transaction.

Pages 173, 174. 15 September 1778. DENNIS O'BRYANT of the county of Henry to JOHN BARKER of same for the sum of thirty five pounds sells 200 acres on the north of Smith River, beginning at a branch. Signed: DENNIS (X) O'BRYANT.

Pages 174, 175. 15 August 1778. JOHN PARR of the county of Henry to WILLIAM BARTON of the same for the sum of seventy five pounds sells 478 acres in Henry County on White Heads Creek, to JOHN FLUCHERS or FLETCHERS line. Signed: JOHN PARR. . . MIRIAM PARR, wife of JOHN PARR relinquishes her right of dower to the above.

Pages 175, 176. 15 August 1778. JOHN PARR of the county of Henry to JOHN FLETCHER of same county for the sum of seventy five pounds conveys 198 acres on White Heads Creek. Signed: JOHN PARR. . .MIRIAM PARR, wife of JOHN PARR relinquishes her right of dower to the above.

Pages 176, 177. 28 September 1778. Relinquish right of dower. ELIZABETH COPLAND, wife of PETER COPLAND relinquishes her right of dower to 7,675 acres of land conveyed to WILLIAM BLACK of Chesterfield County.

Pages 177, 178. Relinquish right of dower. JOHN DANIEL, SR. by his indenture sold to ALEXANDER HUNTER land in Henry County, 179 acres and SARAH DANIEL, wife of JOHN DANIEL, SR. doth hereby relinquish her right of dower.

Pages 178, 179. 19 October 1778. GEORGE HAMILTON of the county of Henry and parish of Camden to ABRAHAM PENN of the same county for the sum of two hundred fifty pounds land on the waters of Beaver Creek by estimate being 680 acres, beginning at the main creek...ANTHONY BILLINGS corner, crossing little Beaver Creek to pointers in JOHN COOPERS line. Signed: GEORGE HAMILTON.

Page 180. 21 October 1778. Entry. JOHN DICKERSON entrees 400 acres land beginning on EDMUND EDWARDS line thence with HUGH CAMBELS line. Also 800 acres in two surveys beginning on the bridge between the head of Dan...Wilson's Creek and the head of Murrels Mull Creek thence about..... Also 800 acres in two surveys beginning where JOHN OLDHAM'S path crosses on...Wagon Road that leads on the ridge between Sandy River waters and Leatherwood waters. Also 400 acres adjoining the line of an entry made by JAMES COX on the Rocky Branch of Sandy River when Run thence of..... Also 400 acres on the Cool Branch of Blackwater River beginning at a Chopt. N.... thence up both sides. Signed: ROBERT WOODS.

Pages 180, 181. 5 November 1778. JAMES RENTFRO of the county of Henry to JOHN RENTFRO of the same for the sum of three hundred pounds land on both sides of Pigg River, it being 300 acres more or less. Signed: JAMES RENTFRO. Wit: PETER VARDEMAN, ISAAC BARTON, DARBY RYAN.

Pages 181, 182. 4 November 1778. We, JOHN RENTFRO, MOSES RENTFRO, ISAAC RENTFRO and JOSHUA RENTFRO are held firmly bound unto JAMES RENTFRO in the sum of three thousand pounds for a tract of land lying on the Pig River that he had formerly conveyed to JOHN HUSK but now sold to JOHN RENTFRO. Signed: JOHN RENTFRO, MOSES RENTFRO, ISAAC RENTFRO, JOSHUA RENTFRO. Wit: WILLIAM RENTFRO, GEORGE RITTURE, JAMES RENTFRO.

Pages 182, 183. 16 November 1778. PETER COPLAND of the county of Henry to ABRAHAM PENN for the sum of one hundred pounds conveys 200 acres more or less on Little Beaver Creek adjoining own land. Signed: PETER COPLAND.

Page 184. 21 September 1778. DAVID HALEY of Henry County to RICHARD COLYAR (COLLYER) of the same for the sum of seven pounds ten shillings sells 10 acres of land in Henry County beginning at the mouth of <u>Boings</u> Creek. Signed: DAVID HALEY.

Page 185. 16 November 1778. ABRAHAM PENN of the county of Henry to JOHN STOKES for the sum of one hundred pounds sells land on Beaver Creek containing 125 acres, it being the land whereon the said STOKES now lives. Signed: ABRAHAM PENN.

Pages 186, 187. 28 May 1778. JOHN ROWLAND and MARY his wife of Henry County to GEORGE HAIRSTON for the sum of two hundred fifty five pounds conveys and sell a tract or parcel of land containing by patent 153 acres more or less on the south side of Smith River...to near Grassy Creek...JOHN BLEVINS line. Signed: JOHN ROWLAND. Wit: ISAAC McDANIEL, <u>BALDIN</u> ROWLAND, HEZEKIAH (X) SALMON.

Page 187. 16 November 1778. Bond of apprentice. Witness that JOSEPH KING in the county of Henry and colony of Virginia hath put his son named JOSEPH KING voluntarily apprentice to WILLIAM TURNER blacksmith in Henry County for a full term of 12 years. The master shall give him one year of training. Signed: JOSEPH KING, WILLIAM TURNER. Wit:

JOHN COLYAR, THOMAS COOPER.

Page 188. Deed of Gift. DAVID HALEY, SR. of the county of Henry colony of Virginia for the love, goodwill and affection which I have and do bare towards my loving son DAVID HALEY, do give a certain tract on the south side of Smith River adjoining COLLYER on the south side and running up said River including all the land on the south side of the River of which before the signing of this present I have delivered him the said DAVID HALEY an inventory signed with my one hand and bearing even date. Signed: DAVID HALEY. Wit: ABRAHAM ADAMS, JOHN COLYAR, JAMES DUNCAN.

Pages 188, 189. 15 February 1779. SAMUEL BIRD of the county of Henry to JOHN HURD of the same county for the sum of one hundred ten pounds land being on both sides of Reede Creek containing 188 acres. Signed: SAMUEL (X) BIRD. . .MARY BIRD, wife of SAMUEL BIRD relinquishes her right of dower to the above.

Pages 190, 191. 25 December 1778. DAVID CHADWELL of the county of Henry and ELIZABETH his wife to JOHN PHILPOTT of the county of Pittsylvania for the sum of one thousand two hundred pounds sells land and all that is on it it being 115 acres on the north side of Irvin (Smith) River...side of B-t-Town Creek, up the said creek east crossing the mouth of Mill Creek. Signed: DAVID (X) CHADWELL, ELIZABETH (X) CHADWELL. Wit: WILLIAM COGGIN, JAMES GODLARD, JAMES (X) MURFEY.

Page 191. 12 October 1778. HUGH ARMSTRONG of the county of Henry to JAMES ARMSTRONG of state of North Carolina and county of Surrey for the sum of one thousand pounds conveys all that tract in Henry County beginning at a poplar in the county line containing 166 acres on both sides of Lovings Creek a branch of the Arrarat River as may appear by patent granted HANNAH CRUNK in the year 1760. Signed: HUGH ARMSTRONG. Wit: JOHN SALMON, JAMES SPENCER, JARROTT PATTERSON, JOHN LINDSEY.

Pages 192, 193. 15 February 1779. PETER COPLAND of Henry County to HENRY HARRIS of the same for the sum of forty pounds sells 86 acres more or less on Reedy Creek. Signed: PETER COPLAND.

Pages 193, 194. 30 December 1778. PETER COPLAND and ELIZABETH his wife of Henry County to JAMES MURPHEY for the sum of seventy pounds land on the branches of Daniels Creek joining MURPHY'S line (no acreage given). Signed: PETER COPLAND. Wit: HARRESON HOBART.

Pages 194, 195. 11 December 1778. JAMES BARROT SOUTHALL and FRANCES his wife of the county of WILLIAMSBURGH to RUBEN NANCE of the county of Henry for the sum of two hundred twenty five pounds conveys a parcel of land containing 400 acres lying in Henry County on the branches of Leatherwood Creek beginning at COLLINGS corner oak...Rocky Branch to BOLING corner oak. Signed: JAMES BARRET SOUTHALL, FRANCES SOUTHALL. Wit: HENRY LYNE, GEORGE HAIRSTON, ABRAHAM PENN.

Page 196. 15 February 1779. WILLIAM HEARD of the county of Henry to AMOS RICHARDSON of the same for the sum of thirty pounds conveys a certain tract or parcel of land containing 399 acres more or less on both sides of Buck Branch in the said county beginning at a poplar in CALDWELL'S line thence on Mirchealer Braylen line. Signed: WILLIAM HURD. Wit: JOHN TURNER, THOMAS PRUNTY, AMOS RICHARDSON.

Pages 197, 198. 15 February 1778. AMOS RICHARDSON of the county of Henry to WILLIAM HEARD, SR. of the same county for the sum of two hundred pounds sells a tract of land on both sides of Reedy Creek containing 230 acres more or less. Signed: AMOS RICHARDSON. Wit: JOHN TURNER, THOMAS PRUNTY, AMOS RICHARDSON, JR.

Pages 198, 199. 8 September 1778. SAMUEL HALL and MILIAN (MILLION, MILLAN) his wife of the county of Henry to PHILLIP RYAN of the same county for the sum of two hundred pounds convey land lying on the south side of Smith River containing by estimate 162 acres, by a mouth of a branch. Signed: SAMUEL HALL, MILLION HALL. Wit: DANIEL REAMEE (RAMY), JOHN ALEXANDER, JR., JOSEPH GOODWIN.

Pages 200, 201. 25 March 1779. PETER HARRIS and HONOUR his wife of the county of Henry to RICHARD MURRILL of the same county for the sum of seven hundred ten pounds, land on north side of Irvin (Smith) River containing by estimate 71 acres ...lines: SAMUEL HOFF, CHARLES WITT'S old patent line, THOMAS HOFF. Signed: PETER HARRIS. . .HONOUR HARRIS, wife of PETER HARRIS relinquishes her right of dower to the above.

Pages 201, 202. 25 March 1779. WILLIAM EASTES of the county of Henry to BENJAMIN COOK, JR. of the same county for the sum of one hundred seventy pounds conveys 60 acres more or less on Snow Creek it being part of a tract of 800 acres granted DAVID CALDWELL by patent bearing date 10 April 1751 and by him to JOSEPH KEATON or JEREMIAH MURROH and by one of them to said WILLIAM EASTIS and divided by a line whereon TULLY CHOICE now lives, being the remaining part of the said tract. Signed: WILLIAM EASTES.

Pages 202. 13 January 1779. Power of Attorney. I, BENJAMIN COOK of Craven County, Camden District, in the state of South Carolina do appoint my son BENJAMIN COOK of Henry County state of Virginia my lawful attorney. Signed: BENJAMIN COOK, SR. Wit: DANIEL RICHARDSON, AARON MACKINZIE, JOHN RAINS (?).

Pages 203, 204. 3 March 1779. DEVERIX GILLIAM and EDY his wife of the county of Henry to SAMUEL STREET for the sum of two hundred fifty pounds convey a parcel of land lying on Homes Creek being by estimate 400 acres. Signed: DEVERIX GILLIAM, EDE GILLIAM. Wit: JAMES EAST, JOSIAH SMITH, THOMAS HAMILTON.

Pages 204, 205, 206. 25 October 1778. WILLIAM HEARD and MARGARETT his wife of the county of Henry to JOHN PINKARD for the sum of seven hundred pounds convey a tract of land being 418 acres more or less; 200 of which the said WILLIAM HEARD bought of RANDOLPH'S executors as by deed recorded in Pittsylvania Court may appear, the other 218 acres bought by said WILLIAM HEARD of AMOS RICHARDSON as by deed recorded in Halifax Court and both tracts are joined together and bounded by lands of HUGH INNES, DANIEL RICHARDSON, HENRY CHUST (?) and RIMINGTON'S old place. Signed: WILLIAM HEARD. Wit: HUGH INNES, HARRY INNES, ANN (X) CHOICE. . .MARGARET HEARD relinquishes right of dower to above.

Pages 206, 207. 15 February 1779. WILLIAM ROBERT HINTON of the county of Henry to PALATIAH SHELTON of the same county for the sum of one thousand eight hundred pounds conveys land and all appertainces on the waters of Russells Creek and of the waters of the Mayo River containing 246 acres adjoining line of JOHN HUNTER. Signed: WILLIAM ROBERT (X) HINTON. Wit: JAMES LYON, DAVID ROGERS, ELIPHAZ SHELTON.

Page 208. Relinquish right of dower. MARY HINTON, wife of WILLIAM ROBERT HINTON, doth relinquish her right of dower to the above transaction.

Pages 209, 210. 15 March 1779. PALATIAH SHELTON and MARY his wife of Henry County to JOSEPH REYNOLDS, son of RICHARD REYNOLDS of Henry County for the sum of two hundred fifty pounds convey and sell 165 acres more or less on both sides of Irvin (Smith) River adjoining line of ROBERT WALTON & Company...crosses a branch. Signed: PALATIAH SHELTON.

Pages 210, 211. 17 April 1779. HENRY MAYS and PHEBEY his wife of Henry County to ABRAHAM MAYS his son, for the sum of forty pounds conveys land situated on the south side of Marrowbone Creek, beginning at the mouth of a small branch on said creek, up said branch to the head, thence south to Haracane branch, thence down to the long branch joining HUGHEY MACCAIN, it being 100 acres more or less. Signed: HENRY MAYES, PHEBE MAYS. Wit: ALEX. McKEEN, WILLIAM MOOR, THOMAS HAMILTON.

Pages 211, 212. 29 April 1779. GEORGE HAIRSTON of the county of Henry to SAMUEL HAIRSTON for the sum of one hundred pounds land containing 228 acres more or less lying on the branches of Nicholes Creek a branch of the north side of Irvin (Smith) River, adjoining PETER SAUNDERS, WILLIAM MEAD, DARBY RYAN, being the survey which was conveyed by ROBERT JONES, JR. to GEORGE HAIRSTON. Signed: GEORGE HAIRSTON.

Pages 213, 214. 22 April 1779. JOHN PACE of the county of Henry to DILLIAN BLEVINS of the same county for the sum of one hundred fifty pounds a tract or parcel of land with all appertances it being 116 acres as may more fully appear by patent granted CHARLES HARRIS. Bounded as follows: corner ash in EDMOND GRAYS & Companys on Smith River, up the same as it meanders to RANDOLPHS & Companys corner white oak. Signed: JOHN PACE.

Pages 214, 215. 8 February 1779. JOSEPH HALE of the county of Henry to JOSEPH PEARSON (PURSON) for the sum of one hundred pounds, sells one hundred acres (100 acres) by patent bearing date at Williamsburgh 20 June 1772, being part of a survey of 233 acres, reference there to being had will more fully appear...situated in Henry County on both sides of Snake Run of Blackwater River and bounded by

Daniels Run where JACOB PRILLIMAN'S new line. Signed: JOSEPH HALE. Wit: ISAAC JONES, ABRAHAM JONES, ISAAC RENTFRO, WILLIAM RENTFRO, THOMAS JONES, JR., JOHN MURPHY. . .REACHAL HALE, wife of JOSEPH HALE relinquishes her right of dower to the above.

Page 216. 22 April 1779. I, EDWARD MURPHY, do certify that I have sold the land I bought of JAMES RENTFRO and took bond for a deed if convenient from JOSEPH HALE and said RENTFRO and that a deed of convaince to JOSEPH PEARSONS shall be a sufficient discharge against the said bond. Signed: EDWARD MURPHY. Wit: JESSE RENTFRO.

Pages 216, 217. 22 April 1779. SHADRACK TURNER of the county of Henry to WILLIAM TURNER of the same for the sum of one hundred pounds conveys land being 20 acres more or less on the south side of Town Creek following the old line according to the pattent to the Creek. Signed: SHADRACK TURNER.

Pages 217, 218. 15 March 1779. SOLOMON DAVIS late of Henry County and WILLIAM CLAY late of Henry County in consideration of the sum of 500..... for a certain dividend of land wherein the above said CLAY doth now live in Henry County beginning at a white oak on JOHN GRIMMETTS line east to a red oak on JOSEPH HODGES line, thence north to a spanish oak on FREDERICK REEVES line, it being 50 acres more or less. Signed: SOLOMON (X) DAVIS. Wit: JAMES COWDEN, SETH BURTON, JAMES MASON, ELISHA KEEN, THOMAS (X) SPALDIN.

Pages 218, 219. 1779. CARRELL KEEN of the county of Henry to ELISHA KEEN of the same for a certain sum of money sells a certain tract of land containing 100 acres more or less lying on Pigg River on the north side, along WILLIAM HALL'S line, THOMAS SPALDIN'S, running along a line of MARKE IRUS to the Pigg River. Signed: CURRELL (X) KEEN. Wit: WILLIAM (X) CLAY, WILLIAM (X) HALL, THOMAS (X) SPALDIN.

Pages 219, 220. 22 April 1779. MOSES RENTFRO of Henry County to PAUL BECK for the sum of one hundred eighty pounds conveys 96 acres lying on the waters of the north fork of the Pigg River. Signed: MOSES RENTFRO.

Pages 220, 221, 222. 31 March 1779. JOHN SMITH of the county of Henry to JOHN HAYNES of the same county for the sum of five hundred pounds conveys 279 acres it being a tract granted JOHN SMITH by patent dated 16 March 1760 situated and lying in the county of Henry and Bedford on both sides of Blackwater River, joining lines of SAMUEL SMITH and WALTON. Signed: JOHN SMITH. Wit: JESSE HEARD, WILLIAM GRAVES, GEORGE HEARD, WILLIAM SWANSON, NATHAN SWANSON.

Pages 222, 223. 25 January 1779. JOHN BOOTH of Henry County and WILLIAMSON COLEMAN of Dinwiddie County to EDWARD SMITH of Pittsylvania County for the sum of four hundred pounds convey land in Henry County by estimate 1,055 acres...lines: MARTIN'S corner; a branch of ROBERTSES Creek thence along STANDFIELD HARDEWAYS line crossing Turkey Cock Creek, JOSEPH LYLLS line. Signed: JOHN BOOTH, WILLIAMSON COLEMAN. Wit: DANIEL HANKINS, JOHN BURCH, GERARD BURCH, HENRY (X) WARRING.

Pages 224, 225. 20 September 1778. JOHN KEEN of the county of Henry to THOMAS SPALDON for a certain sum of money convey 150 acres more or less in Henry County lying and being upon Pigg River on the north side, joining CURRELL KEEN'S line, WILLIAM HALL, LUKE HARDAIN, JOSEPH HODGES, WILLIAM RUN (RYAN?). Signed: JOHN KEEN.

Page 225. 8 April 1779. JOSEPH PEARSON of the county of Henry to JOHN ARTHUR of the same for the sum of eight hundred eighty pounds conveys 174 acres by patent bearing date at Williamburgh 20 June 1772 being a part of a survey of 233 acres, being on both sides of Snake Run of Blackwater River and beginning at Daniel's Run where JACOB PRILLAMAN'S new line takes off. Signed: JOSEPH PEARSON.

Pages 225, 226, 227, 228. 7 November 1778. JACOB CRIST, heir of HENRY CRIST, and ELIZABETH CRIST widow of said HENRY CRIST to SAMUEL LUTTRELL for the sum of two hundred pounds convey 260 acres on Keaton's Creek of Snow Creek beginning at RANDOLPH'S line, CALDWELL'S line and JOSEPH CATON'S line. Signed: JACOB (X) CRIST, ELIZABETH (X) CRIST. Wit: HUGH INNES, THOMAS PRUNTY, WILLIAM RUSSELL, DANIEL LUTTRELL.

Page 228. 15 April 1779. Deed of Gift. I, JOHN WITT of Henry County for good causes, goodwill and affection I bear my son JESSE WITT of Henry County bequeath to him and his heirs all my estate real and personal. Signed: JOHN WITT. Wit: JOSEPH

MORRIS, SAMUEL C. MORRIS.

Pages 228, 229, 230. 27 May 1779. WILLIAM HARDMAN of the county of Henry to JOHN RICHARDSON of the same county for the sum of two hundred pounds to sell and convey land containing by estimate 100 acres it being the land where upon HARDMAN lives, beginning at a hickory on Marrowbone Creek to TAYLOR'S old order line. Signed: WILLIAM HARDMAN. Wit: JAMES TAYLOR.

Pages 230, 231. 15 March 1779. JOHN MATLOCK of the county of Birk and state of North Carolina to ZACAHARIAH SMITH of the county of Henry and state of Virginia for the sum of ninety five pounds sell land on Fall Creek by estimate 50 acres joining JOURNYCAN'S line. Signed: JOHN MATLOCK. Wit: DRURY SMITH, WILLIAM HAYES, JOHN (X) JOURNYKIN, THOMAS SMITH.

Pages 231, 232. 10 February 1779. ZACHARIAH SMITH of Guilford County and state of North Carolina to SHEROD MAYES of the county of Henry state of Virginia for the sum of fifteen pounds convey 76 acres more or less beginning at an oak in JOURNYKIN'S line. Signed: ZACHARIAH SMITH. Wit: DRURY SMITH, THOMAS SMITH, JOHN (X) JOURNYKIN.

Pages 232, 233. 10 February 1779. ZACHARIAH SMITH of the county of Guilford and state of North Carolina to JOHN JOURNYKIN of Henry County, Virginia for the sum of fifteen pounds conveys 75 acres more or less beginning at a line in JOURNYKIN'S own line. Signed: ZACHARIAH SMITH. Wit: DRURY SMITH, THOMAS SMITH, SHEROD (X) MAYES.

Pages 233, 234. 27 May 1779. AMOS RICHARDSON of the county of Henry to JOHN RICHARDSON for love and affection AMOS RICHARDSON has for his son JOHN RICHARDSON gives him a certain parcel of land being 100 acres on Buck branch, a branch of Snow Creek adjoining lines of DAVID PREWIT and TULLY CHOICE. Signed: AMOS RICHARDSON. Wit: WILLIAM RYAN.

Pages 234, 235. 27 May 1779. AMOS RICHARDSON of the county of Henry to LEONARD TARRANT for the sum of one hundred pounds conveys land containing 199 acres on Grassey fork of Snow Creek. 150 acres was surveyed by WILLIAM SIMS the 13 October 1751 as by platt will more fully appear, being bounded within the lines of WILLIAM RYAN and AMOS RICHARD-

SON, JR. Signed: AMOS RICHARDSON. Wit: WILLIAM RYAN.

Pages 236, 237. 26 May 1779. AMOS RICHARDSON of the county of Henry to LEONARD TARRANT for the sum of fifty pounds conveys 50 acres on the Grassey fork of Snow Creek adjoining lines of WILLIAM RYAN and BENJAMIN CHANDLER. Signed: AMOS RICHARDSON. Wit: WILLIAM RYAN. . .Wife (not named) of AMOS RICHARDSON relinquishes her right of dower to the above.

Page 237. 27 May 1779. Bond. Sheriff's Bond of JOHN SALMON by GEORGE HAIRSTON, WILLIAM RYAN, JOHN ROWLAND, WILLIAM TUNSTALL, JESSE HEARD and JOHN COX. JOHN SALMON is to collect the taxes imposed on persons property.

Pages 238, 239. 28 April 1779. THOMAS HAMILTON of the county of Henry to JAMES TAYLOR of the same for the sum of four hundred pounds conveys land more or less 100 acres lying and being in Henry County being part of the land of THOMAS HAMILTON. Beginning on Marrowbone Creek at the mouth of Sinking Creek thence down Marrowbone Creek to the mouth of a branch which is GEORGE ROWLAND'S line. Signed: THOMAS HAMILTON. Wit: JOHN MARR, JESSE CHANDLER, DANIEL TAYLOR.

Page 240. 24 June 1779. WILLIAM MULLINS of the county of Henry to THOMAS HILL of the same for the sum of twenty five pounds conveys 70 acres more or less on the east fork of Town Creek of the Smith River, being part of a tract granted WILLIAM MULLINS by patent 5 March 1773. Signed: WILLIAM MULLINS. . .JEAN MULLINS, wife of WILLIAM MULLINS, relinquishes her right of dower to the above.

Pages 241, 242. 24 June 1779. WILLIAM MULLINS of the county of Henry to JOHN MULLINS for the sum of ninety pounds sells 70 acres more or less on the east fork of Town Creek of the Smith River...THOMAS HILL'S line mentioned. Signed: WILLIAM MULLINS. . .JEAN MULLINS, wife of WILLIAM MULLINS relinquishes her right of dower.

Pages 242, 243. 24 June 1779. JOHN RAMSEY of the county of Henry and parish of Patrick to THOMAS WARREN for the sum of one hundred pounds sells land on the north side of the north fork of Chestnut Creek being part of a tract granted JOHN RAMSEY by patent 10 August 1759 which contains 75 acres more or less. Signed: JOHN (X) RAMSEY.

Page 247. 25 June 1779. At a Court held for Henry County the above receipt from JOHN FREDERICK MILLER to ROBERT WADE, JR. was proved by the oath of witnesses thereto to be the act and deed of J. F. MILLER. Signed: JOHN COX.

Pages 247, 248. 25 August 1779. SAMUEL STREET and his wife (not named) of the county of Henry to DANIEL WILSON for the sum of one thousand pounds conveys 400 acres of land lying and being in the said county on both sides of Home Creek. Signed: SAMUEL STREET.

Pages 249, 250. 15 August 1779. THOMAS MILLER of the county of Henry to JOHN WILSON of the county of Botetourt of the state of Virginia for the sum of one hundred fifty pounds sells 150 acres of land it being the same as by patent bearing date at Williamsburgh 15 June 1773, reference thereto being had will more fully appear, situated in Henry County on both sides of the main...south of Blackwater River. Signed: THOMAS (X) MILLER. . .ELIZABETH, the wife of THOMAS MILLER relinquishes her right of dower to the above.

Pages 250, 251. 22 July 1779. MILLER DOGGETT of the county of Henry to THOMAS HILL of the same county for the sum of five hundred pounds conveys land and appertainces on both sides of Pigg River containing 97 acres. Signed: MILLER DOGGETT. Wit: A. HUGHES, WILLIAM COOK, PETER SAUNDERS, JOSEPH EAST, DANIEL ROSS, H. WOODS, SWINFIELD HILL.

Page ?. 20 March 1779. Apprenticeship Bond. JOSEPH CHANDLER of the parish of Patrick and county of Henry to REUBEN PAYNE of the same. JOSEPH CHANDLER doth hereby place and bind ROBERT CHANDLER an apprentice to said REUBEN PAYNE to dwell and continue and serve from this date until he arrives at the age of twenty-one years, he now being twelve years old since 12 of April last. In turn REUBEN PAYNE will teach him to read, wright and cypher. Signed: JOSEPH CHANDLER, REUBEN PAYNE. Wit: JOHN GEORGE, JOHN EAST.

Pages 253, 254, 255. 18 January 1779. GEORGE HAMILTON of the county of Henry to ALEXANDER MOORE the son of WILLIAM MOORE of the state of North Carolina and the county of Gilford for the sum of one hundred twenty pounds conveys land by estimate to be 250 acres more or less according to a survey lately made, on Marrowbone Creek...to a branch which divides the land from JESSE CHANDLER. Signed: GEORGE HAMILTON, MARY HAMILTON, his wife. Wit: JOSEPH ANTHONY, ALEXANDER MCKEEN, HUGH MCKEEN.

Pages 255, 256. 6 May 1779. Deed of Trust. WILLIAM BROWN and JAMES WILLIAMS of the county of Henry to JOHN MINTER for the sum of eight hundred thirty four pounds ten shillings, which JOHN MINTER acknowledges himself indebted, honestly desires to secure and pay them and for and in further consideration of five shillings like money paid to JOHN MINTER by said BROWN & WILLIAMS. MINTER sells to WILLIAM BROWN and JAMES WILLIAMS a negro fellow named Bob and a negro girl named Fanny. Signed: JOHN MINTER. Wit: IGNATIOUS SIMMS, GEORGE HAIRSTON, SAMUEL LANIER.

Page 258. Relinquish right of dower. JOSEPH PEARSON sold to JOHN ARTHUR 175 acres of land and now ELIZABETH PEARSON, wife of JOSEPH PEARSON relinquishes her right of dower to the transaction.

Page 258. 21 April 1779. Deed of Trust. Be it known to whom it may concern that we, JOSEPH FARGUSON and PATIENCE his wife for consideration of ANN FRAZIER GATEWOOD taking out a certain suit now depending in Henry Court for sundry negros that we do by consent give up the said negros to the said ANN FRAZIER GATEWOOD to her and her heirs forever...only in the...consideration that the said ANN FRAZER GATEWOOD do lend to her mother PATIENCE FARGUSON two of the same during her natural life, named Will and Render and then at her death (PATIENCE) to return the said to ANN FRAZIER GATEWOOD as hers. Signed: JOSEPH FARGUSON, PATIENCE FARGUSON. Wit: WATERS DUNN, JR., JOHN TINCH.

Pages 259, 260. 27 July 1779. JOHN BOHANON of the county of Henry to ROBERT PRUNTY for the sum of fifty pounds conveys land on both sides of Pigg River being 50 acres more or less...pointers in the old line on the south side of Pigg River. Signed: JOHN (X) BOHANON. Wit: FREDERICK REEVES, THOMAS HALE, ELISHA EASTES, THOMAS PRUNTY.

Pages 260, 261. 17 July 1779. ROBERT BOULTON of the county of Henry to WILLIAM VINSON for the sum of thirty seven pounds sells 200 acres of land on both sides of Snow Creek beginning at a oak in THOMAS BOULTON'S line, thence to a white oak at the corner of PHILLIP BLESSINGHAM'S. Signed: ROBERT

Pages 261, 262. 17 July 1779. ROBERT BOULTON of the county of Henry to AMOS RICHARDSON for the sum of thirty five pounds conveys 200 acres more or less on Snow Creek beginning at the falls on the north side of the creek to WILLIAM VINSON'S line, thence to a patent line. Signed: ROBERT BOULTON.

Pages 262, 263. 24 March 1779. ROBERT BOULTON of the county of Henry to JOSIAH BROCK of the county of Bedford for the sum of one hundred fifty pounds conveys 300 acres more or less on both sides of Snow Creek beginning at the patent line to WILLIAM WEBB'S. Signed: ROBERT BOULTON. Wit: MARY (X) BOULTON, ANN (X) BOULTON.

Pages 264, 265. 4 March 1779. THOMAS MURRELL of the county of Henry to JEFRAY MURRELL of the same county for the sum of thirty pounds conveys land being 400 acres on Muster Branch of Leatherwood Creek. Beginning at Lomax & Company's corner poplar in a small branch. Signed: THOMAS MURRELL. Wit: WILLIAM TUNSTALL, MARVEL NASH, BENJAMIN MURRELL.

Pages 265, 266. 26 August 1779. WILLIAM LOVELL and his wife (not named) to JOHN DAVIS of Henry County conveys a parcel of land being the one half of 150 acres more or less whereon I now live, beginning at a new line on JOSEPH GRAVELLY'S line at a dead post oak, thence along the new line to Hooker Branch, down it as it meanders to the mouth of Jones' Spring Branch, to JOHNSON'S line. Signed: WILLIAM LOVELL.

Page 267. 22 July 1779. PETER VARDEMAN of the county of Henry to DANIEL SPANGLE for the sum of one hundred pounds land on both sides of Pigg River being 65 acres more or less on the north side...to Hatchett Run...on the north side of the River of PHIPSES PATEN or tract. Signed: PETER VARDEMAN. Wit: JAMES COWDEN, THOMAS HALE, WILLIAM COOK, JOHN TURNER, HENRY (X) BARKSDALE.

Pages 268, 269. 20 August 1779. WILLIAM LOVELL of the county of Henry to NICHOLAS AKIN for the sum of twenty pounds sells land on the waters of Leatherwood Creek 75 acres more or less. Lines: JOSEPH GRAVELY, Hooker's branch, Jones' Spring Branch, FRANCIS COX'S. Signed: WILLIAM LOVELL.

Pages 269, 270. 29 August 1779. PHILIP RYAN of the county of Henry to WILLIAM SWANSON for the sum of one thousand pounds sells 1,062 acres lying on the south side of Smith River...corner line of RANDOLPH'S and others. Signed: PHIL. RYAN.

Pages 271, 272. BARNET HEARD to JESSE HEARD for the sum of fifty five pounds sells 805 acres being part of a tract containing 1,712 acres granted to STEPHEN HEARD by patent bearing date 29 May 1760, situated and lying in the county of <u>Halifax</u> on the waters of Blackwater River. Signed: BARNET HEARD.

Pages 272, 273. 26 August 1779. Bond. Bond of ABRAHAM PENN, HENRY LYNE, GEORGE HAIRSTON and ALEXANDER HUNTER. Purpose: ABRAHAM PENN is constituted and appointed escheator for the said Commonwealth of the said county of Henry. ABRAHAM PENN will and truly account for and pay all sums of money that he shall receive from the states (?) of British property in the said county.

Pages 273, 274. 27 October 1779. CHRISTIAN ROADS of the county of Henry to JOHN FARGUSON, SR. for the sum of ten thousand pounds sells land on both sides of Pigg River...beginning on the north side of the River...(no acreage given). Signed: CHRISTIAN ROADES. . .ELIZABETH, the wife of CHRISTIAN ROADES relinquishes her right of dower.

Pages 275, 276. 27 October 1779. JAMES TAYLOR of Henry County to JOHN WILBURN of the county of Powhatan for the sum of four hundred pounds sells 100 acres more or less it being a tract said JAMES TAYLOR had from THOMAS HAMILTON; beginning on Marrowbone Creek at the mouth of Sinking Branch to a branch that was GEORGE ROWLAND'S line. Signed: JAMES TAYLOR.

Pages 276, 277. 11 March 1779. JOHN WOODSON of the county of Cumberland state of Virginia and ELIZABETH his wife to JOHN WATSON of the county of Montgomery and state of Maryland for the sum of one hundred eighty pounds sells 950 acres of land in Henry County, formerly part of Pittsylvania County on both sides of Horsepasture Creek a branch of the Mayo River, which said land is bounded as is expressed and comprived in certain letters. Patent granted to said WOODSON for same land bearing date at Williamsburgh 1 March 1773. Signed: JOHN WOODSON, ELIZABETH WOODSON. Wit: JOHN ABINGTON, BOWELES ABINGTON, LUCY ABINGTON.

Page 278, 279. 20 October 1779. DAVID MATLOCK of the county of Henry to WILLIAM LOVELL for the sum of sixty pounds conveys 197 acres on Reed Creek, the plantation whereon the said MATLOCK now resides. Lines: WILLIAM HEARD, ARIS VAUGHAN, HENRY VAUGHAN. Signed: DAVID MATLOCK. Wit: RICHARD NEWPORT, JOSEPH (X) GRAVELY, DAVID WATSON. . .MARGARET (MARGET) MATLOCK, wife of DAVID MATLOCK relinquishes her right of dower to the above.

Pages 279, 280. 15 April 1779. PETER COPLAND and ELIZABETH his wife to ABRAHAM PENN for the sum of seven hundred pounds sells land lying and being on the branches of Little Beaver Creek, by estimate 750 acres. Lines: beginning in Penn's corner red oak, THOMAS COOPER'S line, ROBERT STOCKTON'S crossing Red Bank Creek. Signed: PETER COPLAND, ELIZABETH COPLAND. Wit: AMBROSE JONES, SALLY COPLAND.

Pages 280, 281. 14 April 1779. PETER COPLAND and ELIZABETH his wife of Henry County to ANTHONY BILLING (BITTING?) for the sum of two hundred pounds sells land being 350 acres more or less. Lines: ROBERT DANIELD, crosses DANIELDS Creek, STOCKTON'S. Signed: PETER COPLAND, ELIZABETH COPLAND. Wit: AMBROS JONES, SALLY COPLAND.

Pages 281, 282. 28 September 1779. JOHN RICE of Pittsylvania County to WILLIAM ALEXANDER of Henry County for the sum of one hundred pounds sells land it being 150 acres more or less in the county of Henry on both sides of Marrowbone Creek. Signed: JOHN RICE, MARY (X) RICE. Wit: SAMUEL BEVINS, CHARLES (X) BEVINS, ABRAHAM ALEXANDER FRANKLING.

Pages 283, 284. 28 October 1779. WILLIAM COX and JEMIMAH COX his wife of the county of Henry to CARR BAILEY of the same for the sum of fifty pounds sells land, etc as may more fully appear in the pattent granted DAVID HALEY in the year 1755 10th September. This land on the south side of Smith River and contains 40 acres. Signed: WILLIAM COX, JEMIMAH COX.

Pages 284, 285. 21 July 1779. PETER COPLAND and ELIZABETH his wife to ROBERT STOCKTON all of Henry County for the sum of two thousand pounds a parcel of land by estimate to be 1,000 acres. Lines: THOMAS COOPER, JOSEPH COOPER, SIMS' line, crosses a branch of Beaver Creek. Signed: PETER COPLAND, ELIZABETH COPLAND. Wit: THOMAS COOPER, JOSEPH

COOPER, JOSEPH GOODWIN.

Pages 286, 287. 17 August 1779. SAMUEL JORDON of the county of Buckingham to JOHN SALMAN of the county of Henry for the sum of eighty five pounds, land in Henry County on Jordon's and Ramsey's Creek, containing by estimate 200 acres more or less; it being part of an order of Council formerly granted to the said SAMUEL JORDON and JACK POWER. Beginning at a pointer in King's line along the dividing line between SAMUEL JORDON and JACK POWER, down Jordon's Creek and Ramsey's Creek. Signed: SAMUEL JORDON. Wit: HENRY SUMPTON, BENJAMIN DILLIN, JAMES SHELTON.

Pages 287, 288. 26 October 1779. JOHN PARR, SR. of the county of Henry to WILLIAM KEATON for the sum of fifty pounds sells 200 acres of land lying and being in Henry County on both sides of Spoon Creek adjoining HAMON CRITZ. Signed: JOHN PARR, SR.

Pages 288, 289. 26 May 1779. JOHN KINDRICK of the county of Henry to BENJAMIN STINNETT for the sum of one hundred pounds sells 100 acres of land on Buffalow Creek, it being the upper part of the said tract whereon I formerly lived. The Stitting (?) branch at upper branch to the beginning... Signed: JOHN KINDRICK, ELIZABETH. Wit: JESSE HEARD, WILLIAM GARDWIN (GARDNER), THOMAS (X) KINDRICK.

Pages 290, 291. 26 May 1779. JOHN KINDRICK of the county of Henry to THOMAS FLOWERS for the sum of one hundred pounds conveys 110 acres on Buffelow Creek, it being the lower part of said tract whereon I formerly lived. Signed: JOHN KINDRICK, ELIZABETH KINDRICK. Wit: JOSEPH HURT, WILLIAM GARDNER, THOMAS KINDRICK.

Pages 291, 292. 23 September 1779. ALEXANDER HUNTER of the county of Henry to ARCHELAUS HUGHES of the same for the sum of twelve hundred pounds conveys 179 acres on the south side of the Mayo River. Signed: ALEXANDER HUNTER.

Pages 293, 294. July 1779. PETER COPLAND of the county of Henry to JOHN CUNNINGHAM of the same for the sum of one hundred sixty pounds sells 225 acres more or less beginning at a white oak sapling near the old Baptist Meetinghouse to WILLIAM ESTES' corner, crosses Reedy Creek. Signed: PETER

COPLAND. Wit: ROBERT COX.

Page 194. 19 January 1778. Bond of JOHN DICKERSON, WILLIAM TUNSTALL and JOHN CAMERON. Purpose: JOHN DICKERSON to be surveyor for the county of Henry.

Page 295. 17 November 1777. Deed of Gift. I, ELLIONER TORBORN of the county of Henry for the sum of four shillings paid by my daughter JINNET MCKINNER but more especially for the love and goodwill I have for my said daughter, I do give my said daughter one horse, a woman's saddle, 4 head cattle, 3 head sheep, 1 feather bed, 6 pewter plates, 3 pewter basins, 1 large pewter dish, 1 large iron pot, 1 dutch oven and their further increase. Signed: ELLIONR (X) TORBORN. Wit: HENRY LYNE, FREDERICK REAVES, JOHN COX.

Pages 295, 296. 24 November 1779. CARR BAILEY and MARY TURNER of the county of Henry to DAVID CHADWELL of the county of Pittsylvania for the sum of 2400 (pounds?) Virginia money do convey land and all that pertains to it containing 40 acres more or less lying and being in the said county of Henry beginning at a beech on the south side of Smith River. Signed: CARR BAILEY, MARY TURNER. Wit: CHARLES BARKER, EDWARD BARKER, WILLIAM ADAMS.

Page 297. November 1779. Power of Attorney. I, MALACHIAH CUMMINGS of the county of Henry for divers good causes hereunto moving have made, ordained and constituted and appointed my trusty friend JACOB ADAMS my true and lawful attorney to act for me to convey to any other person a certain tract of land lying on Town Run in the county of Fauquier containing 46 acres. Signed: MALACHIAH (X) CUMMINGS.

Pages 298, 299. 13 July 1779. BENJAMIN COOK, JR. attorney for BENJAMIN COOK, SR. and MARY COOK his wife, to THOMAS THRELKELD of the county of Henry sell him land and all that it contains for the sum of four hundred eighty two pounds containing 100 acres and being on both sides of Snow Creek and joins DANIEL RICHARDSON'S mill. Signed: BENJAMIN COOK, MARY COOK. Wit: JOHN PINKARD, AARON MCKENZIE, DANIEL RICHARDSON.

Pages 300, 301. 17 June 1779. JOHN DONELSON and RACHEL his wife of the county of Washington to JAMES CALLAWAY and JEREMIAH EARLY of the county of Bedford for the sum of four thousand pounds sells two tracts of land situated in Henry County, one of which tract lies on both sides of a branch of Pigg River called Iron Mine Branch containing 400 acres adjoining ROBERT HILL. The other tract of parcel of land conveyed to said DONELSON by FRANCIS BYRD as by deed recorded in the county court of Pittsylvania, reference being thereunto will appear containing 200 acres more or less. Signed: JOHN DONELSON, RACHEL DONELSON. Wit: JAMES THOMPSON, MARY INNES, ALEXANDER DONELSON, H. HENRY, JR., CALEB TATE, SWINFIELD HILL, MORDECAI MASSEY.

Pages 302, 303, 304. 25 June 1779. Relinquish right of dower. To: WILLIAM CAMPBELL and ISAAC SHELBY or any two justices of the peace of Washington County. JOHN DONELSON has conveyed land by estimate 600 acres in Henry County and his wife cannot conveniently travel to same, please obtain relinquishment of dower. . .Justices replied they had received said relinquished of right of dower from RACHEL DONELSON.

Pages 304, 305. 11 November 1779. PETER COPLAND of the county of Henry to MARVEL NASH for the sum of one thousand pounds sells 1,000 acres of land beginning at a chestnut in the old order line, to another old line to AMBROSE JONES and JOSEPH COOPER'S lines, to an elm on Beaver Creek. Signed: PETER COPLAND. Wit: AMBROSE JONES.

Pages 306, 307. 25 November 1779. PETER COPLAND of the county of Henry to JOHN PYRTLE of the same for the sum of one hundred fifty pounds, money of Virginia conveys 250 acres more or less on Reedy Creek, joins CUNNINGHAM'S corner...to near the old meetinghouse. Signed: PETER COPLAND.

Pages 307, 308. 10 November 1779. PETER COPLAND of the county of Henry to HENRY VAUGHAN of the same for the sum of thirty five pounds conveys land on the branches of Reedy Creek containing 300 acres more or less. Signed: PETER COPLAND. Wit: THOMAS COOPER, JOHN KITCHIN, MICAJAH ANTHONY.

Page 309. 24 November 1779. HENRY VAUGHAN of the county of Henry to JOHN RENO of the same for the sum of one hundred pounds conveys a parcel or tract of land on the branches of Reedy Creek it being 100 acres more or less adjoining lines of JORDAN and LOVENS. Signed: HENRY (X) VAUGHAN.

Page 310. 2 October 1779. Inquisition. Inquisition indented, taken and held by A. PENN ESCHEATOR for the said county of Henry at GEORGE WALLER'S Esquire on Smith's River in said county. By the oaths of JOHN WILLS foreman and JOHN HARDMAN, GEORGE ROWLAND, PHILIP THOMAS, JAMES ANTHONY, JAMES TAYLOR, JOHN STOKES, JOHN MCCONWAY, PHILIP RYAN, JAMES MEREDITH, JOHN BARKSDALE and DILLION BLEVINS good and lawful men of said county who were impannelled and returned by JOHN SALMON, GENT. SHERIF of said county who after hearing evidence openly in presence of said ESCHEATOR and SHERIF and upon their oaths do say: That a tract or parcel of land containing 1150 acres being an undivided part of 2300 acres belonging to RANDOLPH, HARMER & KING lying in said county on Smith River, Jordon's Creek and Mayo River bounded by the known an established lines thereof is at present held as the estate of JOHN HARMER and WALTER KING who are British subjects and ought to vest in the Commonwealth according to the Act of Assembly intitled an "An Act Concerning ESCHEATS & Forfeitures from British Subjects". In witness whereof the said ESCHEATOR and Jurors their hands and seals to two endentures of this Tenor and date here set. Signed: A. PENN, Esch., JOHN WILLS. (The above juror signed...JOHN MCCONWAY signed JOHN CONWA).

Pages 311, 312. Inquisition. Inquisition taken by A. PENN ESCHEATOR for Henry County at JOHN WELL'S on Leatherwood Creek by oath of JOHN WILLS, foreman, JOHN PINKARD, DANIEL RICHARDSON, AMOS RICHARDSON, SPENCER CLACK, JAMES MORTON, SAMUEL LUTTRELL, REUBIN NANCE, JOHN WYATT, JOHN MCCONWAY, GEORGE HAIRSTON and JOHN DAVIS. The above do say: That tracts or parcels of land containing 4695 acres lying on Marrowbone Creek, Doe Run and the branches of Pigg River and Doe Run and branches of Leatherwood Creek known by established lines thereof is held as the estate of JAMES SMITH who is a British subject and ought to vest in the Commonwealth. (Signed by the above with the exception of JOHN MCCONWAY).

Pages 312, 313. Inquisition. Taken at JOHN WELLS' on Leatherwood Creek by oaths of GEORGE HAIRSTON, foreman, JOHN PINKARD, DANIEL RICHARDSON, AMOS RICHARDSON, SPENCER CLACK, JOEL ESTES, RUBIN NANCE, JOHN MCCONWAY, SAMUEL PATTERSON, JAMES MORTON, JOSEPH LEWIS and SAMUEL LUTTRELL. That 1,665 acres being the tenth part of 16,650 acres lying on Leatherwood Creek undivided belonging to THOMAS LOMAX, THOMAS MAN RANDOLPH, and JOHN HARMER and WALTER KING.

1,500 acres in Fall Creek and Middle Creek, 1,000 acres on the south branches of Reed Creek at present held in the estate of said JOHN HARMER and WALTER KING who are British subjects.

Pages 313, 314. Inquisition. Inquisition of a British Subject. At GEORGE WALLER'S on Smith River with JOHN WELLS, foreman, JOHN HARDMAN, GEORGE HAIRSTON, PHILIP THOMAS, JAMES ANTHONY, JAMES TAYLOR, JOHN STOKES, JOHN MCCONWAY, PHILIP RYAN, DILLION BLEVINS, JAMES MEREDITH and JOHN BARKSDALE. Two tracts of land containing 1,600 acres on both sides of Blackberry Creek and on the south side of Smith River and the other containing 1,200 acres on Marrowbone Creek at present held as the estate of WALTER KING, British subject.

Pages 314, 315. Inquisition. Inquisition held at GEORGE WALLER'S on Smith River JOHN WELLS, foreman (with the same persons as pages 313, 314 as jurors)...850 acres more or less lying on both sides of Beaver Creek on the north side of Smith or Irvin River, held in the estate of PATRICK COUTTS, deceased heirs who is a British subject.

Pages 315, 316. Inquisition. Held at JOHN WELLS on Leatherwood Creek. GEORGE HAIRSTON, foreman, JOHN PINKARD, DANIEL RICHARDSON, AMOS RICHARDSON, SPENCER CLACK, JOEL ESTES, RUBIN NANCE, JOHN MCCONWAY, SAMUEL PATTERSON, JAMES MORTON, JOSEPH LEWIS. Two tracts 496 acres more or less on both sides of Marrowbone Creek and Doe Run is at present held in the estate of ARCHIBALD SMITH a British subject. Dated 1 October 1779.

Pages 316, 317. Held at WATERS DUNN'S on Marrowbone Creek by oath of JOHN MARR, foreman, ANDREW RAY, GEORGE ROWLAND, DILLION BLEVINS, SAMUEL LANIER, JOHN HARDMAN, THOMAS COOPER, JAMES TAYLOR, PHILIP RYAN, PHILLIP THOMAS, JAMES MEREDITH and JOHN MANNING. 2300 acres more or less on both sides Marrowbone Creek, also one other parcel on both sides of Horsepasture Creek containing 2,700 acres held by the estate of JOHN HARMER, British subject.

Pages 318, 319. 25 November 1779. Bond. Bond of JOSEPH ALLSOP and JOHN COX to the Justices of Henry County in the amount of one thousand five hundred pounds, the condition of the bond being that JOSEPH ALSOP is the administrator of the estate of THOMAS GARNER, deceased.

Page 319. 25 November 1779. Bond. JOSIAS SHAW and GEORGE HAIRSTON bond for the sum of fifty pounds. JOSIAS SHAW has obtained license to keep an ordinary at his house in Henry County. Therefore, SHAW shall constantly find and provide in his said ordinary good, wholesome and cleanly lodging and diet for travellers and stableage fodder and provender as the season shall require for their horses for and during the term of one year. Shall not suffer or permit any unlawful gaming in his house, nor on the Sabbath suffer any person to tipple or drink anymore than is necessary.

Pages 320 thru 340 are blank.

Pages 340 thru 346 surveys.

A List of Surveys made by JOHN DICKERSON.

YEAR 1778

When	No.	For Whom	Place
Mar 19	1	WILLIAM STEPHENS	branches of Home Creek
Mar 20	1	JOHN SAMS	branches Turkey Cock of Smith River
Mar 21	1	HUGH CAMBRIL	Turkey pin a branch of Matrimony Creek
Apr 23	1	HAMON CRITZ, SR.	Mill Crk of Mayo River
Apr 24	1	ANTHONY SMITH	North side of No. Mayo River whereon he now lives
Apr 25	1	JAMES SHELTON	Horsepasture Creek
Apr 28	1	JOSEPH ROBERTS	North Mayo River
Jun 5	1	JOHN DILARD	Horsepasture Creek
Jul 21	1	BAYNES CARTER	Ready Crk
Jul 30	1	AMOS RICHARDSON	Grassy fork of Snow Crk
July 31	1	WILLIAM LONG	a branch of Snow Crk
Nov 18	1	MARTIN KEY	Smith River in Harmer & King's order
Nov 24	1	WILLIAM YOUNG	1st fork of Snow Crk
Nov 25	1	WILLIAM YOUNG	inclusive on Snow Crk both sides
Nov 26	1	STEPHEN SENTER	branches of Turkey Cock Crk
Nov 26	1	WILLIAM HAYNES	Dinner Crk at North branch of Pigg River
Nov 27		JOHN ELLIS	inclusive on branches of Bull Runn & Jacks Crk
Nov 28		NATHAN SWANSON	Waters of Bull Run

Date		Name	Location
Nov. 30	2	JOSIAH KIRBY	inclusive on Owens Crk & Pole Cat branch
Dec 1		JOHN DICKERSON	Cool branch of Blackwater R.
Dec 2		LUKE HUGINGS	branch of Bull Run
Dec 2		THOMAS CARTER	on Blackwater River
Dec 3		PHILLIP RAITEY	on a branch of Bull Run
Dec 4		BEN MCCRAW	on Bull Run
Dec 5		JOHN KEMP	Blackwater R. and branches
Dec 7		ISMAEL STANDIFER	Standifer branch of Blackwater
Dec 5		JAMES STANDIFER, SR.	Blackwater and branches
Dec 7		ISRAEL STANDIFER	Standifer's branch adj. the former
Dec 8		STEPHEN HEARD	branch of Blackwater & Poplar Camp branch
Dec 9	4	STEPHEN HEARD	Poplar Camp & Cedar Run
Dec 11		STEPHEN HEARD	Poplar Camp on Blackwater River
Dec 10		STEPHEN HEARD	branches of Blackwater
Dec 13		JOHN LUMSDAN	branches of Blackwater River
Dec 16		PHILLIP BLASHINGHAM	on Snow Creek
Dec 17		MICHAEL DUNN	Back branch & Gutting Run of Snow Crk.

1779

Date		Name	Location
Jan 1		THOMAS PRUNTY	on Snow Creek waters
Jan 11		JESSE CLAY	on Blackwater River
		JOHN STEWART (?)	on Blackwater River
Jan 12		PETER GILLIUM	on Blackwater River
Jan 26		THOMAS BLACK	on Snow Creek
Feb 2		JOHN LUMSDEN	branches of the maple swamp on Blackwater River
Feb 3		JOHN HEARD	Maple swamp & Robertsons branch of Pigg River
Feb 4		ROBERT HILLS Excs.	Waters of Chestnut Crk
Feb 5		Same	on Pigg River
Feb 6		SWINFIELD HILL	on Pigg River
Feb 8		ROBERT HILLS Excs.	Same
Feb 10		GEORGE HEARD	on waters Poplar Camp Crk
Feb 24		THOMAS PRUNTY	Mountain Crk at Pigg R.
Feb 24		WILLIAM VINCENT	Bucks branch of Snow Crk
Feb 26		PHILLIP RAILEY	including former surveys and land whereon he now lives
Feb 27		JOHN DAVIS	Owens Crk of Pigg R. waters
Mar 3	6	EARLY & CALAWAY	Pigg R. & Blackwater R.
Mar 5	2	Same	south branch Pigg R.
Mar 5		THOMAS HALE	branch of Pigg R.
Mar 10		JAMES CALLAWAY	branches Chestnut Crk
Mar 11		ROBERT HILL Excs.	branches of Blackwater near grave yard
Mar 12		Same	south branches Pigg R.
Mar 30		AARON & ABRAHAM FONTON	order council on Crooked Creek & Mayo Rd.
Apr 6		WILLIAM MEAD	on Bulls Run
Apr 7		PHILLIMON SUTHERLAND	Same
Apr 12		EDWARD RICHARDS	north fork Chestnut Crk
Apr 13		JAMES COOLEY	Same
Apr 13		JOHN HARGER	Same
Apr 15		JOHN FARGUSON	Pigg River
Apr 15		CHRISTIAN ROADS	Story Crk of Pigg R.
Apr 16		THOMAS HILL	south side Pigg R. adj. own lines
Apr 17		EARLY & CALLAWAY	on bold nobb Mores entry
Apr 16		SOLOMAN DAVIS	south side Pigg R.
Apr 17		EARLY & CALLAWAY	north branches Pigg R.
Apr 19		ROBERT HILL Excs.	on Meadow Crk.
Apr 20		JAMES STANDEFER, JR.	Story Crk waters
Apr 20		SAMUEL RENTFROW	Same
Apr 26		ROBERT HILL Excs.	McDowell's branch
Apr 27		Same	both sides Blackwater R.
Apr 27		JOHN & JOSEPH EARLY	branches Blackwater R.
Apr 28		ROBERT HILL Excs.	Robertson's branch
Apr 29		WILLIAM COOK	on Hatchett Run
Apr 30		HENRY JONES	north branches Pigg R.
Apr 30		DARBY RYAN	same
Apr 30		WILLIAM MAVITY	same
Apr 30		PHILLIP SHERIDEN	north fork Storey Crk
May 1		JAMES STANDIFER, SR.	on Story Crk

Date	Name	Location
May 1	WILLIAM WEEKS	same
May 1	WILLIAM MAVITY	same
May 3	WILLIAM BOHANNON	head of Town Crk
May 3	JOHN DICKERSON	south fork Story Crk
May 4	JAMES STANDIFER, SR.	head of Story Crk
May 5	JACOB ATKINS	north fork Story Crk
May 5	MILTON DOGGETT	Pigg River
May 6	PETER VARDEMAN	south side Pigg R.
May 6	DARBY RYAN	Pigg River
May 7	OWEN RUBELL	branches Pigg R.
May 7	ROBERT JONES	same
May 7	JOEL RAGLAND	Turnors Crk
May 8	JAMES TARPINE	branches Hatchett Run
May 10	JOHN WILLIS	Hatchett Run & branches
May 10	Same	Same
May 10	HENRY WILLIS	a branch of Blackwater
May 12	THOMAS MILLER	south fork Blackwater
May 11	STEPHEN LEE	branch of Blackwater
May 11	PETER HUFF	south fork Blackwater
Jun 3	WILLIAM FARGUSON	south fork Pigg R.
Jun 3	PAUL BECK	north fork Pigg R.
Jun 4	JOEL RAGLAND	same
Jun 5	ROBERT MAVITY	Nicholases & Otter Crk.
Jun 5	WILLIAM DUNN	on branch of Pigg R.
Jun 5	WILLIAM MAVITY	on Turner's Crk.
Jun 5	DAVID JONES	Nicholas' or Otter Crk.
Jun 7	CAPT. THOMAS JONES	Turner's & Nicholases Crk.
Jun 7	JOHN JONES	Nicholases Crk.
Jun 8	MICHAEL REAL	Same
Jun 8	PETER GEARHEART & LEWIS	on Hatchett Run
Jun 8	WILLIAM DAVIS	Story Crk.

Pages 1, 2.   24 February 1780. JAMES SHELTON of the county of Henry for and in consideration of divers good causes and more especially for the natural love and affection that I have for my son WILLIAM SHELTON, do give him one tract or parcel of land containing by estimate 200 acres more or less adjoining the land of GREGORY DURHAM, SAMUEL COLEMAN MORRIS and JOHN DILLARD. Beginning at a poplar where my land SAMUEL SHELTON'S and JOHN DILLARD'S corner. Signed: JAMES SHELTON. Wit: JOHN BARKSDILL, HENRY BARKSDILL, ISAAC SMITH. . . .Possession granted 24 February 1780. Signed: JAMES SHELTON. Wit: JOHN DILLARD, RANDOLPH HALL, GREGORY DURHAM.

Pages 2, 3.   24 February 1780. JAMES SHELTON to SAMUEL SHELTON. That the said JAMES SHELTON for and in consideration of a bay stallion sells unto SAMUEL SHELTON a certain parcel of land containing 130 acres more or less in the county of Henry on both sides of Horsepasture Creek, it being part of a tract of land the said JAMES SHELTON purchased of THOMAS MANN RANDOLPH. Lines: beginning at a tree between the said JAMES SHELTON, WILLIAM SHELTON and JOHN DILLARD on the north side of Horsepasture Creek, also joins JOSIAH SMITH. Signed: JAMES SHELTON. Wit: JOHN DILLARD, WILLIAM SHELTON, GREGORY DURHAM.

Pages 4, 5.   24 February 1780. JAMES SHELTON of Henry County for divers good causes and especially for the love and affection that I have for my son-in-law GREGORY DURHAM give unto him a parcel of land containing 150 acres more or less on both sides of Ironmonger Creek adjoining lands of WILLIAM SHELTON, SAMUEL COLEMAN MORRIS and JAMES SPENCER. Beginning at a corner on SAMUEL C. MORRIS' line, WILLIAM SHELTON'S, north side of Little Horsepasture Creek to the mouth of Ironmonger back to Little Horsepasture Creek as it meanders to a Hornbeam. Signed: JAMES SHELTON. Wit: JOHN DILLARD, RANDOLPH HALL, WILLIAM SHELTON.

Page 6.   3 February 1780. THOMAS JONES of the county of Henry to MICHAEL REEL of the same for the sum of thirty pounds conveys land on the headwaters of Nicholas Creek and Story Creek containing 242 acres, it being a part of a larger tract. Signed: THOMAS JONES. Wit: JOSHUA RENTFRO, WILLIAM STANDEFER, JOSEPH JONES, ISAAC JONES.

Page 7. 24 February 1780. Bond. Bond of ARCHELOUS HUGHES as sheriff of Henry County to collect from every tithable person the sum of three pounds in the said county. Secureties: WILL. TUNSTALL, ABRAHAM PENN, MORDECAI HORD and GEORGE HAIRSTON.

Page 8. 24 February 1780. Bond. A. HUGHES appointed Sheriff of the county of Henry shall well and truly collect all officers fees and dues put into his hand to collect. Securities same as above.

Page 9. 25 November 1779. PETER COPLAND of the county of Henry to WILLIAM ESTES of the same for the sum of two hundred pounds a parcel of land it being 200 acres more or less...crosses Reedy Creek joins CUNNINGHAM'S line. Signed: PETER COPLAND. Wit: JAMES ANTHONY, GEORGE DANIEL, JAMES (X) COURSEY.

Pages 10, 11. 28 May 1777. GEORGE LUMPKINS and MARY his wife of Henry County to HENRY MAYSE of same county for the sum of seventy five pounds conveys land on the south side of Marrowbone Creek beginning at the mouth of Spring branch at CHANDLER'S corner then up the branch which is the line between LUMPKIN and MAYSE and along said MAYSES' line to said LUMPKIN'S old order line to Harrican branch which is HENRY MAYSE'S line containing 271 acres. Signed: GEORGE LUMPKINS. Wit: THOMAS HAMILTON, ALEXANDER MCKEEN, THOMAS MCKEEN.

Pages 11, 12. 18 September 1780. Dower Release. ISRAEL STANDEFER has sold to RICHARD EDMUNDSON 404 acres of land and SUSANNAH the wife of said ISRAEL STANDEFER hereby relinquishes her right of dower.

Pages 12, 13. 21 September 1779. JONATHAN PRATT of the county of Henry to HUMPHREY BURDITT of Pittsylvania county for the sum of seventy five pounds conveys 79 acres of land, it being part of a patent granted JOHN SMITH 16 March 1775...joins COWEN'S line to the mouth of Bull Run. Signed: JONATHAN PRATT. Wit: WILLIAM BURDETT, JOHN PRATT, JARVASS BURDITT.

Pages 13, 14. 23 March 1778. JOHN MINTER of the county of Henry to THOMAS COOPER for the sum of eight hundred thirty four pounds and ten shillings which the said JOHN MINTER is justly indebted to the said COOPER and desires to pay him and for and in further consideration of the sum of five shillings doth grant and sell to COOPER one negro man slave named Bob and one negro girl named Fanny. Signed: JOHN MINTER.

Pages 15, 16. 23 March 1780. MICHAEL ROWLAND of the county of Henry to ALEXANDER HUNTER of the same for the sum of six hundred pounds conveys and sells land on the Smith River containing 400 acres more or less. Signed: MICHAEL ROWLAND. . .ELIZABETH ROWLAND, wife of MICHAEL relinquishes her right of dower.

Pages 16, 17. 6 September 1780. SAMUEL BOLLING of the county of Henry and his wife ABI to GUY SMITH of the county of Bedford for the sum of one hundred fifty pounds sell land on Snow Creek in the amount of 207 acres, it being part of a 400 acre tract by patent granted TULLY CHOICE 16 September 1775 and conveyed by TULLY CHOICE to SAMUEL BOLLING by deed 28 March DCCLXXI beginning at WILLIAM HALL'S corner in the old line. Signed: SAMUEL BOLLING, ABI (X) BOLLING. Wit: EUSEBUS HUBBARD, AMOS RICHARDSON, PHILIP BLASSINGAME.

Pages 17, 18. 6 September 1779. JAMES RENTFRO of the county of Henry to WILLIAM COOK of the same for the sum of ten pounds conveys land on both sides of Pigg River on the north fork of the said River, being part of a tract granted by patent to ROBERT JONES, SR. in 1753, containing 12 acres. Signed: JAMES RENTFRO. Wit: JOSHUA RENTFRO, ISAAC JONES, LEONARD (X) GEARHEART, PETER GEARHEART.

Pages 18, 19. 22 March DCCXXX. WILLIAM VINCENT and his wife MARY of the county of Henry to PHILIP BLASSINGAME for the sum of thirty five pounds convey land beginning at a beech on THOMAS BOULTON'S line near Snow Creek. Signed: WILLIAM VINCENT, MARY (X) VINCENT. Wit: BIRD SMITH, AMOS RICHARDSON, EUSEBUS HUBBARD.

Pages 20, 21. 12 March 1780. WILLIAM MAVITY of the county of Henry to JOEL RAGLAND of the county of Goochland for the sum of fifty pounds sells land in the amount of 193 acres by grant bearing date at Williamburgh 8th November in the 4th year of the Commonwealth, refer thereto will more fully show details. Being on both sides THOMAS JONES' Mill Creek and SMITH'S line. Signed: WILLIAM MAVITY. Wit: WILLIAM FARGUSON, DAVID JONES, ELIJAH JONES.

Pages 21, 22. 23 March 1780. ELISHA ESTES and FRANCIS his wife of the county of Henry and parish of Patrick to BOTTOM ESTES for the sum of one hundred five pounds conveys land on Camp Branch, being 100 acres more or less joins lines of JOHN WILKS, according to patent. Signed: ELISHA ESTES, FRANCIS EASTIS.

Pages 22, 23. 27 October 1779. WILLIAM SWANSON, SR. of the county of Henry to PHILIMON SOUTHERLAND of the same for the sum of six hundred pounds conveys 150 acres on both sides of Bull Run, beginning at WILLIAM SWANSON JR'S. corner red oak to WALTON'S, to HAYNE'S, CLARKSON'S to NATHAN SWANSON'S line. Signed: WILLIAM SWANSON. Wit: NATHAN SWANSON, JOHN SWANSON, WILLIAM SWANSON, JR.

Pages 23, 24. Deed of Trust. I, NATHANIEL KETCHUM of the county of Henry to WILLIAM BARTEE convey two certain horses, one called Jimcrack and a white horse. Condition of this obligation is that if the above NATHANIEL KETCHUM do deliver unto WILLIAM BARTEE one certain continental horse marked and branded, which horse the said BARTEE give a receipt to ALEXANDER BROWN LEE on the value thereof then the above obligation to be void, otherwise remain in effect. Signed: NATHAN KETCHUM. Wit: JOHN LINDSAY, JAMES LINDSAY.

Pages 24, 25. 22 February 1780. MARTIN KEY of Fluvannah County, attorney for WALTER KING of the Kingdom of Great Britian of the one part and WILLIAM GRAVES of the county of Henry of the other part, whereas the said KING by his certain letter of attorney dated 1777 empowering MARTIN KEY to sell and dispose of certain lands on the south side of Smith River in Henry County. The said KEY did convey and sell unto WILLIAM GRAVES 150 acres on the south side of Smith River for the sum of seventy five pounds. Signed: MARTIN KEY. Wit: JOHN ALEXANDER, THOMAS BUSH, DANIEL REAMY.

Pages 26, 27. 27 January 1778. DILLION BLEVINS of Henry County to WILLIAM GRAVES for the sum of one thousand pounds conveys land, all messuage, tenement, tract or parcel of land with the appurtences on the south side of Smith River adjoining the other lands of said WILLIAM GRAVES purchased of the said BLEVINS containing 116 acres by patent granted CHARLES HARRIS. Joins a corner oak of EDMUND GRAY & Company on Smith River thence up the River as it meanders unto RANDLOPH & Company. Signed: DILLION BLEVINS. Wit: GEORGE HAIRSTON, ALEXANDER HUNTER, JOHN COX. . .The above recorded 27 January 1780.

Pages 27, 28. 23 March 1780. That is that GEORGE HAIRSTONE under-Sherif of the county of Henry shall during his continuance in office well and truly execute the said office and in all things appertaining or in anywise belonging to the office of Sherif, keep safe and indemnified the aforesaid ARCHELAUS HUGHES him and his heirs and from all cost and damages that may in anywise accure from misconduct, malpractice or breach of office, also due payment make of all moneys, tobacco or what may be from time to time by law required. Signed: GEORGE HAIRSTONE, AB. PENN, HENRY LYNE. Wit: ALEXANDER HUNTER, JAMES SPENCER.

Pages 28, 29. 25 March 1780. JOHN SALMON to GEORGE WALLER for the sum of twenty pounds land containing 10 acres beginning at a large poplar on Jordon's Creek near the lower end of SALMON'S Plantation to a line where the dividing line between JORDON and POWERS crosses a branch called McCutchins branch. Signed: JOHN SALMON.

Pages 29, 30. 25 March 1780. NATHANIEL KETCHAIM of the county of Henry to MICHAEL ROWLAND for the sum of two thousand pounds land on both sides of the North Mayo River being part of a tract formerly held by JOSEPH ROBERTS, deceased, conveyed to him by THOMAS RANDOLPH, Esq. which will fully appear by record in the General Court, being part of a tract whereof ELIZABETH ROBERTS, now ELIZABETH KETCHAIM was seized of at the time of her marriage with the said NATHANIEL KETCHAIM. Beginning on the said river above the plantation whereon the said ELIZABETH lived thence to run as to leave the plantation houses, orchards, still and still house in the possession of the said ROWLAND so as to leave out the two upper fields and river together with the woodlands above the hills. Signed: NATHANIEL KETCHAIM.

Pages 31, 32. 27 April 1780. JOHN ROWLAND of the county of Henry to JOHN MINTER for the sum of one hundred sixty five pounds land on the branches of Leatherwood Creek being 240 acres more or less joining LOMAX and ACUFF lines. Signed: JOHN ROWLAND. Wit: JOHN WELLS, WILL. BLEVINS, GEORGE HAIRSTONE.

Pages 32, 33. 1780. JOHN ROWLAND, SR. of the county of Henry to JOHN ACUFF for the sum of five hundred pounds land, tenament being 40 acres more or less on Leatherwood Waters joins lines of LOMAX, JOHN MINTER and ACUFF. Signed: JOHN ROWLAND. Wit: GEORGE HAIRSTONE, JOHN WELLS, WILL. BLEVINS.

Pages 34, 35. 25 April 1780. THOMAS JONES to WILLIAM STANDEFER for the sum of one hundred pounds 260 acres tenament, land or tract on the waters of Nicholas Creek in Henry County, crosses Storey Creek, CHOATS line. It being by estimation the said produces 266 acres. Refers to previous deed. Signed: THOMAS JONES. Wit: LUKE STANDEFER, JOSEPH JONES, STEPHEN LEE, WILLIAM STANDLEY.

Pages 35, 36. 20 April 1780. JOSEPH SHORES PRICE and CHARITY his wife of the county of Buckingham and WILLIAM DANDRIDGE of the parish of St. Martin and county of Hanover for the sum of six thousand pounds a tract of land in Henry County containing by estimate 530 acres more or less beginning on the north side of Marrowbone Creek. Signed: JOSEPH SHORES PRICE. Wit: ARCHIBALD BOLLING, THOMAS LORTON, JANE BOLLING.

Page 37. 4 December 1779. WILLIAM HAMMOND and SALLEY his wife of the county of Henry to ROBERT BOLTON for the sum of eight hundred fifty pounds land on the north side of Pigg River containing 1,000 acres more or less joins WILLIAM HAYNES. Signed: WILLIAM HAMMON. Teste: ANN (X) BOLTON (BOULTON), ELIZABETH (X) BOULTON, WINEY (X) WEBB, ROBERT BOULTON, JR., ROBERT PERRYMAN.

Pages 38, 39. 1 June 1779. ISRAEL STANIFER of the county of Henry to RICHARD EDMONSON of the same for the sum of fifty pounds conveys one tract of land containing 404 acres, it being the tract on which the said I. STANDEFER lived, lying on the south side of Blackwater on Stanifer Creek which was granted ISRAEL STANIFER by patent dated 1774. Signed: ISRAEL STANDEFER, SUSANNAH STANDEFER. Teste: RICHARD PERRYMAN, JESSE HEARD, GEORGE HEARD.

Pages 40, 41. 25 November 1779. PETER COPLAND to THOMAS JAMESON for the sum of two hundred pounds conveys land containing 600 acres more or less beginning at HARRIS' corner on Reedy Creek. Signed: PETER COPLAND. Wit: JOHN JAMESON, JOHN NORRIS, WILLIAM BROWN.

Page 41. 4 January 1780. Deed of Gift. I, JOSEPH FITZPATRICK of the county of Fluvannah for the natural love and affection I bear my grandson WILLIAM HORD, son of GEORGE HEARD of the county of Henry, I give and bequeath to said child, an infant, one negro girl named Agnes and if you don't make him equal to his mothers part of my estate at my decease, my estate shall be properly divided by executors and him made equal with ye rest of my children. Signed: JOSEPH FITZPATRICK. Wit: JESSE HEARD, PETER (X) HOLLAND, WILLIAM (X) STEWART, WILLIAM (X) BLANKINSHIP.

Pages 42, 43. 27 April 1780. WILLIAM HUNTER of the county of Henry to JOHN HUNTER of the same for the sum of one hundred pounds convey land containing 160 acres more or less on Butterum Creek of Smith River, beginning with WILLIAM STANDLEY'S lower line, then down both sides of said creek following the old line as low as the island ford to a new line for quantity it being part of a tract of land granted to SHIM COOK by patent 16 February 1771. Signed: WILLIAM HUNTER.

Pages 43, 44. 6 November 1779. PETER COPLAND of the county of Henry to RICHARD COPLAND of the same for the sum of three hundred fifty pounds conveys land in the amount of 150 acres beginning at a chestnut in Buffalo Gapt to the foot of the mountain. Signed: PETER COPLAND. Wit: AMBROSE JONES, WILLIAM JONES, ROBERT STOCKTON.

Pages 44, 45. 25 April 1780. Apprentice Bond. Bond between ANTHONY SMITH, a Blacksmith of Henry County and ANN HOOPER. This day ANN HOOPER put her son WILLIAM HOOPER as an apprentice to the said ANTHONY SMITH to serve as an apprentice until WILLIAM arrives at the age of 21 years which the said WILLIAM will be on the 1st day of January 1791. WILLIAM HOOPER promises to keep his masters secrets, not contract matrimony, shall not frequent taverns nor play at any unlawful game, shall not by or sell without special license of his Master. The said ANTHONY SMITH shall endeavor to teach WILLIAM HOOPER the blacksmith trade and give him one years schooling, give sufficient meat, drink, apparell, washing and lodging fit for an apprentice. Signed: ANTHONY SMITH, ANN HOOPER. Wit: JOHN DILLARD, RANDOLPH HALL, MILES JENNINGS.

Pages 46, 47. 13 December 1779. JOHN SMITH and MARTHA his wife of the county of Guilford and state of North Carolina to THOMAS LEVISTON of the county of Henry state of Virginia for the sum of forty five pounds convey to LEVISTON 3/4ths of that messuage tract or parcel of land in Henry County on Blackwater containing by estimate 58 acres. It was granted by patent to the said JOHN SMITH 28 July 1768. The above 3/4ths granted to be held in common with JAMES SANDEFER, JR. he having obtained this by deed from JOHN & MARTHA SMITH for the 1/4th part of the above 58 acres. Signed: JOHN SMITH, MARTHA SMITH. Wit: JOSEPH JONES, MARK RENTFROE, GRIMES (X) HALKUM.

Pages 47, 48. 13 December 1779. JOHN SMITH and MARTHA his wife of the county of Guilford and state of North Carolina to JAMES STANDEFER of the county of Henry for the sum of fifteen pounds sell 1/4th part of a tract of land in Henry County on the branches of Blackwater River containing by estimate 58 acres (see deed above pages 46, 47) to be held in common with THOMAS LEVISTON the owner of the 3/4th part. Signed: JOHN SMITH, MARTHA SMITH. Wit: JOSEPH JONES, MARK RENTFRO, GRIMES (X) HALKUM.

Pages 49, 50. 27 May 1780. JAMES POTEET of the county of Henry to NATHAN HALL of the same for the sum of twenty pounds conveys 234 acres more or less adjoining the tract of land where HALL now lives upon which he purchased formerly of the said POTEET, joins the Smith River. Signed: JAMES POTEET.

Pages 50, 51. 25 May 1780. JAMES POTEET of the county of Henry to BENJAMIN HUBBARD of the same for the sum of twenty pounds sells and conveys 216 acres of land beginning at a chestnut on PEDEGOW'S (PEDIGO) line also a white oak on DANIEL RYAN'S line. Signed: JAMES POTEET.

Pages 51, 52. 25 May 1780. PETER COPLAND of the county of Henry to ROBERT CAVE for the sum of twenty five pounds conveys and sells land in Henry County it being 50 acres more or less, joins WILLIAM HEARD, WILLIAM ESTES and Reedy Creek. Signed: PETER COPLAND. Wit: JOHN CUNNINGHAM, JOHN HEARD, THOMAS (X) JONES, ARIS (X) BAUGHAN.

Pages 53, 54. 10 December 1779. JEFFERY MURREL and MARTHA his wife to GEORGE REYNOLDS all of the county of Henry conveys for the sum of one thousand pounds 400 acres on Muster branch of Leatherwood Creek adjoining Lomax & Company line corner. Signed: JEFFERY MURRELL, MARTHY MURRELL. Wit: JOSEPH CROUCH, JOHN CROUCH, WILLIAM STEPHENS, BENJAMIN MURRELL.

Pages 54, 55. 9 February 1780. ELISHA WALKER of the county of Pittsylvania to JOHN JINKINS of the county of Henry for the sum of two hundred pounds sells 100 acres more or less of land on the south side of Pigg River. Signed: ELISHA WALKER. Wit: THOMAS SMITH, LEWIS JINKINS, WILLIAM JINKINS.

Pages 55, 56. 27 April 1780. THOMAS HILL of the county of Henry to THOMAS RAY sells for the sum of seventeen pounds sells land being 70 acres more or less on the east fork of Town Creek of Smith River, being part of a tract granted WILLIAM MULLINS by patent 1 March 1773. Signed: THOMAS HILL. Wit: WILLIAM HUNTER, EDGCOME GWILLMES, JOHN (X) KISTERSON.

Pages 57, 58. 22 May 1780. JONATHAN HANBY of the county of Henry to EDWARD TATUM of the same for the sum of forty pounds sells a certain tract of land beginning at HANBY'S corner, crosses two branches, it being part of a tract granted JONATHAN HANBY and DAVID HANBY by patent 15 June 1773. Signed: JONATHAN HANBY. Wit: JAMES LYON, MARY (X) HENSLEY.

Pages 58, 59, 60. 1779. DAVID HANBY to JONATHAN HANBY for the sum of two hundred pounds conveys a tract of land in Henry County containing 964 acres on both sides of Peters Creek. Recorded: 25 May 1780. Signed: DAVID HANBY.

Page 60. 25 May 1780. WILLIAM TAYLOR of the county of Henry to DRURY SOLAMON conveys 160 acres of land on both sides of Bull Run adjoining lands of JOHN HARMER for the sum of one hundred pounds. Signed: WILLIAM TAYLOR.

Pages 61, 62. 25 May 1780. JOSIAH CARTER of the county of Henry to THOMAS ROBINSON for the sum of one hundred pounds conveys lands, tenemants, etc on both sides of Blackwater River as may appear by patent granted JOSIAH CARTER containing 200 acres. Signed: JOSIAH CARTER.

Pages 62, 63. 25 May 1780. ISAAC MCDONALD of the county of Henry to GEORGE MABRY for the sum of two thousand pounds sells a tract of land lying on the south fork of Rock Castle Creek containing 150 acres with all appurtenances. Signed: ISAAC MCDONALD. . .MARY, the wife of ISAAC MCDONALD relinquishes her right of dower.

Page 64. 25 May 1780. ISAAC MCDONALD of the county of Henry to JONATHAN ISON of the same for the sum of eighty pounds good and lawful money of Virginia do sell and grant unto said ISON land in the fork of Rock Castle Creek containing 5 acres more or less beginning at corner of BENJAMIN KINZEY to line of GEORGE MABRY. Signed: ISAAC MCDONALD.

Page 65. 25 May 1780. ISAAC MCDONALD to BENJAMIN KINZEY, JUNR. for the sum of forty pounds sells land on the north fork of Rock Castle Creek containing 144 acres, joins GEORGE MABRY and on the dividing ridge between the south and north fork to JONATHAN ISON'S corner. Signed: ISAAC MCDONALD. MARY MCDONALD, wife of ISAAC relinquishes her right of dower.

Page 66. 25 May 1780. PETER COPLAND of the county of Henry to IGNATIOUS SIMMS for the sum of eighty pounds sells 100 acres of land beginning at a white oak in ROBERT STOCKTON'S line on the bank of a fork of Beaver Creek called Simms' Creek also joins line of THOMAS COOPER. Signed: PETER COPLAND.

Page 67. 25 May 1780. Bill of Sale. THOMAS BOTTOM of the county of Amelia of the one part sells to PATTY RIVES of the county of Henry of the other part for the sum of one hundred pounds sells and delivers one negro girl named Edy. Signed: THOMAS BOTTOM. Wit: FREDERICK RIVES, ALEXANDER RIVES.

Page 67. 25 May 1780. Bill of Sale. JOHN HILTON of the county of Henry sells and delivers unto THOMAS HENDERSON one negro woman slave named Jries for the sum of two thousand pounds. Signed: JOHN HILTON. Wit: JOHN HENDERSON, JAMES (X) SHORT.

Page 68, 69. 25 May 1780. JOHN MARR, GEORGE ROWLAND and JOHN ROWLAND, SR. all of Henry County to JOSIAS SHAW for the sum of ten thousand two hundred pounds sell land in Henry County whereon the said SHAW now lives containing 600 acres more or less beginning on MACAIN'S corner in TAYLOR'S order line, on Marrowbone Creek to the falls of the said creek, along HIXES line to the schoolhouse branch to MORE'S corner. Signed: JOHN MARR, GEORGE ROWLAND, JOHN ROWLAND. Wit: WILL. TUNSTALL, DAVID LANIER, REUBIN PAYNE, THOMAS BEDFORD.

Page 69. 25 May 1780. JOHN MARR and GEORGE ROWLAND of the county of Henry to JOSIAS SHAW sell and convey 2 acres of land on the north side of Marrowbone Creek beginning at the Falls. Signed: JOHN MARR, GEORGE ROWLAND.

Page 70. 25 May 1780. Bond. JOSIAH CARTER, JOHN FONTAINE and JESSE HEARD are held bound to the Justices. The condition of the above obligation is such that if the above bounded JOSIAH CARTER shall on or before the last day of September next coming build or erect or cause to be built and erected a Courthouse at the place appointed by the Justices of Henry County of the following dimisions to be the Courthouse 24 feet by 20 feet, round logs laid close, hewd within side 9 foot pitch from floor to floor. The lower floor to stand 2½ feet from the ground, said house to be covered with square peg shingles 21" long with one window above and two below stairs, shuters to said windows. The floors to be planked in plain close form. Two doors strongly made, one attorney's bar strongly fixed, proper seats for attorney and Jury also a proper bench for the Court to sitt also a seat and box for the Sherif and a table 4 foot long and 3 foot wide with a drawer in said table proper for the use of the Clerk. Which work is to be done strongly and of sound timber by the time above mentioned on the true performance of which the above obligation to be void otherwise remain in full force power and virtue. Signed: JOSIAH CARTER, JESSE HEARD, JOHN FONTAINE. Wit: HAYNES MORGAN.

Page 71. 25 May 1780. THOMAS HAMBLETON and MARY his wife of the county of Henry to GEORGE ROLING (ROWLAND?) for the sum of two thousand pounds sells and conveys land on the north side of Marrowbone Creek beginning at the mouth of Sinking branch to TAYLOR'S corner, SHAW'S line, LANIER'S line to LEMUEL LANIER'S line containing 300 acres more or less. Signed: THOMAS HAMILTON. Wit: JOHN BARKSDILL, P. HAIRSTON, SAMUEL HAIRSTON, MICHAEL ROWLAND.

Page 72. 25 May 1780. Receipt. Received of Mr. JOHN MARR one thousand seven hundred pounds it being the full of the within consideration. Signed: THOMAS HAMILTON.

Pages 72, 73. 26 April 1780. ABRAHAM PENN of the county of Henry to JOHN COOPER for the sum of one hundred pounds sells a 300 acre tract of land on Beaver Creek joining ANTHONY BITTINGS, crosses little Beaver Creek to JOHN COOPER'S line. Signed: ABRAHAM PENN.

Pages 73, 74. 19 June 1780. WILLIAM MAVITY of the county of Henry to JOHN KINSY for the sum of two hundred pounds sells and conveys 366 acres of land it being by grant bearing date at Williamburgh 20 October 1779. On the north branch of Pigg River. ..JONES' old line, HILL'S corner, to on top of the Whirling Hill. Signed: WILLIAM MAVITY. Wit: DAVID JONES, EDWARD TATUM, ELIJAH JONES.

Pages 75, 76. 22 June 1780. EDMUND LYNE of the county of Henry to ALEXANDER HUNTER for the sum of six hundred pounds sells and conveys land on the south side of Irvin or Smith River, it being part of the tract of land known by the name of the Horse Shoe which said LYNE purchased of THOMAS M. RANDOLPH containing by estimate 400 acres. Signed: EDMUND LYNE. Wit: HENRY LYNE, ROBERT TATE, JOHN CAMERON (X).

Pages 76, 77. 22 June 1780. EDMUND LYNE of the county of Henry to JOHN MARR, GEORGE HAIRSTON and THOMAS BEDFORD for the sum of seven thousand pounds grant, sell and convey land on the north side of Irvin or Smith River by estimate 260 acres, it being part of the tract known by the name of the Horse Shoe which said LYNE purchased of THOMAS RANDOLPH. Signed: EDMUND LYNE. Wit: HENRY LYNE, ROBERT TATE, JOHN (X) CAMERON.

Page 78. 25 April 1780. ROBERT BOLTON of the county of Henry to WILLIAM HAYMES (HAYNES) for the sum of seventy five pounds conveys and sells land on both sides of Pigg River containing 244 acres beginning at the River on BOLTON'S line, LAW'S corner, GRAVE'S line, YOUNGS' line, POTTER'S line, HAMMONS line. Signed: ROBERT BOLTON.

Page 79. 22 June 1780. ROBERT BOLTON and MARY his wife of the county of Henry to ROBERT POWELL for the sum of one hundred pounds sells land on the south side of Pigg River containing 152 acres. Signed: ROBERT BOLTON.

Page 80. 24 February 1780. JOHN INGRUM and ELIZABETH his wife of the county of Henry to BLACKMORE HUGHES of the same for the sum of twenty pounds sells and conveys 200 acres more or less on the north side of Irvin River. Signed: JOHN INGRUM, ELIZABETH INGRUM. Wit: JOHN DICKENSON, PETER HARRIS, THOMAS JONES, JR.

Pages 81, 82. 22 February 1780. MARTIN KEY of the county of Fluvannah attorney in fact for WALTER KING of Great Britian to MORDECAI HOARD of the county of Henry. KEY being appointed in 1777 to dispose of land on both sides of Smith River does for the sum of seven hundred pounds sell and convey unto said HOARD 1,750 acres on both sides of Smith River to the ancient known and established bounds thereof and which was a larger tract granted by patent to RANDOLPH, HARMER & KING. Signed: MARTIN KEY. Wit: JOHN ALEXANDER, DANIEL REAMEY, THOMAS BUSH.

Pages 83, 84. 26 July 1780. WILLIAM STANDEFER of the county of Henry to DARBY RYAN for the sum of two thousand pounds sells and conveys all lands and tenements being 266 acres on the Draught of Smith River and bounded by patent dated 20 October 1779 also by dividing line between JONES and REEL also by deed from THOMAS JONES to WILLIAM STANDEFER. Signed: WILLIAM STANDEFER. Wit: JOS. JONES, WILLIAM YOUNG, ISAAC BARTON.

Pages 84, 85. 26 July 1780. DARBY RYAN of the county of Henry to JOSEPH JONES for the sum of three thousand pounds sells land and messuages on both sides of Pigg River containing 50 acres one tract and 54 acres in the other joining line between JONES and BARTON. Signed: DARBY RYAN.

Page 86. Dower right. ELIZABETH INGRUM wife of JOHN INGRUM relinquishes her right of dower to Justices as she can not conveniently travel to the Courthouse.

Pages 86, 87. 27 July 1780. ROWLAND CHILES of Henry County to JOHN INGRAM for the sum of thirty pounds sells 110 acres of land beginning at a corner elm of THOMAS FINNEY'S on the upper side of Butterham Town Creek to a tree on the north side of Smith River. Signed: ROWLAND CHILES, NANCY CHILES. Wit: P. HAIRSTON, ABRAHAM PAYN, REUBIN PAYNE. . . NANCY CHILES, wife of ROWLAND relinquishes right of dower.

Page 88. 13 June 1780. WILLIAM YOUNG of the county of Pittsylvania to DAVID WILLIS of Henry County for the sum of one hundred fifty pounds sells and conveys 198 acres on Little Sycamore Creek. Signed: WILLIAM YOUNG.

Pages 89, 90. 27 July 1780. WILLIAM RENTFRO of Henry

County to JOHN PEAK of the same for the sum of fifty pounds sells land on the south side of Rennett Bag Creek it being 45 acres more or less. Signed: WILLIAM RENTFRO.

Pages 90, 91. 30 March 1780. MORDECAI HOARD and SARAH his wife of the county of Henry to PATRICK HENRY for the sum of five thousand pounds sell and convey land on the north side of Smith River and adjoining thereto and on both sides of Mulberry Creek containing 350 acres more or less according to ancient and known and established bounds which said MORDECAI HOARD purchased from MARTIN KEY, attorney for WALTER KING of Great Britian and lately rented to WILLIAM GARDNER who lived on the same the last year and joins JOSEPH BOULDING and JOHN FONTAINE. Signed: MORDECAI HOARD. Wit: JOHN KING, SAMUEL GATES, WILLIAM ALEXANDER.

Pages 92, 93. 26 July 1780. WILLIAM YOUNG of Henry County to WILLIAM STANDEFER of the same for the sum of two thousand pounds sells and conveys 232 acres of land on the Pigg River. Signed: WILLIAM YOUNG.

Pages 93, 94. 27 April 1780. Dower right. PETER COPLAND sold land to ABRAHAM PENN and ELIZABETH COPLAND who cannot conveniently travel to the Courthouse relinquishes her right of dower to the Justices.

Pages 95, 96. Dower Right. PETER COPLAND sold land to ROBERT STOCKTON (1,000 acres) and as ELIZABETH wife of PETER COPLAND cannot conveniently travel to the Courthouse, the Justices secure her relinquishment of dower.

Page 97. Dower Right. Justices secure release of dower right of OBEDIENCE, wife of PHILIP RYAN who conveyed land to WILLIAM SWANSON, SR. it being 160 acres.

Pages 97, 98. 25 December 1779. THOMAS BOULDIN of the county of Charlotte to JOHN WILLIAMS of Henry County for the sum of eighty pounds sells land on both sides of the south side of the south fork of Leatherwood Creek it being 200 acres. Signed: THOMAS BOULDIN. Wit: RALPH MITCHELL, MATTHEW (X) CLEMENT, PATRICK (X) MCBRIDE.

Page 99. 4 June 1780. STEPHEN HEARD to JOHN SHORT

for the sum of one hundred pounds sells 170 acres of land on Blackwater River, joins HEARD'S old line to PETER HOLLAND'S line. Signed: STEPHEN HEARD. Wit: WILLIAM TRENT, HENRY TRENT, JOHN TRENT.

Pages 100, 101. 27 July 1780. JOHN MARTIN of the county of Henry to OBADIAH GRAVITT for the sum of one hundred pounds sells and conveys land on the fall branch of Chestnut Creek containing 100 acres. With the order line held by ROBERT WOODS and said MARTIN, LUKE THORNTON'S Mill path. It being part of the order of council held by the said ROBERT WOODS & JOHN MARTIN. Signed: JOHN MARTIN.

Pages 101, 102. 24 August 1780. ROBERT WOODS of Henry County to JOHN MARTIN of the same, whereas the said ROBERT WOODS and ROBERT WEEKLEY being in partnership in an order of council of 4,600 acres of land on Chestnut Creek the same granted to WOODS & WEEKLEY selling his part thereof unto said JOHN MARTIN and ROBERT WOODS on Chestnut Creek to a Mill Dam occupied by JACOB STOVER.

Page 102, 103. 24 August 1780. Bond of Apprentice. FOSTER DOBBS son of JOHN DOBBS of the county of Henry doth put himself apprentice unto THOMAS JAMESON, Blacksmith, to serve him from the day and the date herefore and during seven years. Signed: THOMAS JAMESON, JOHN (X) DOBBS, FOSTIN (FOSTER) (X) DOBBS. Wit: DAVID LANIER, REUBIN PAYNE.

Page 104. 19 August 1780. PETER COPLAND of the county of Henry to DANUEL JACKSON for the sum of two hundred twenty pounds sells 100 acres of land more or less beginning at a small branch of Beaver Creek, joins IGNATIUS SIMMS' corner. Signed: PETER COPLAND.

Page 105. 25 May 1780. Dower right. JONATHAN HANBY did convey unto EDWARD TATUM 300 acres of land and as his wife SARAH HANBY cannot conveniently travel to the Courthouse, the Justices secure relinquishment of right of dower.

Page 106. 29 September 1780. Bill of Sale. WILLIAM GARDNER of the county of Henry for the sum of three thousand pounds sells and delivers unto BALDWIN ROWLAND one negro man named Lall. Signed: WILLIAM GARDNER. Wit: GEORGE ROWLAND, JOHN COX.

I, HENSON GARDNER of Montgomery County have bargained,

sold to BALDWIN ROWLAND of Henry County my right and title for one negro fellow. Signed: HENSON GARDNER. Wit: JOHN BARKSDILL, BRICE MARTIN.

Page 107. 16 Aug 1780. JEREMIAH SALSBURY of the county of Henry to MATHEW AGEE of the same for the sum of two hundred pounds sells 171 acres of land on Blackwater River beginning at JAMES STANDEFER'S corner. Signed: JEREMIAH (X) SOUSBURY.

Pages 108, 109. 19 June 1780. SARAH HUTCHERSON to SAMUEL PATTERSON for the sum of fifty pounds sells 50 acres of land, it being within the lines of JOEL ESTES and THOMAS THRAILKELD and SAMUEL PATTERSON'S own lines. Signed: SARAH (X) HUTCHENSON. Wit: WILLIAM RYAN, ABRAHAM PENN, FREDERICK RIVES, THOMAS PRUNTY.

Page 109. 27 August 1780. Bill of Sale. To OBEDIENCE RYAN for seven pounds ten shillings for a negro girl named Fillis which I have made mention of in my last will and testament. Signed: JOHN ROWLAND. Wit: ELIZABETH NUNN.

Page 110. Agreement between JOSIAH CARTER and BAYNES CARTER in the amount of three thousand pounds being indebted to BAYNES CARTER by vardict of a Jury sent out by Cort to view the jacent land above the said JOSIAH CARTER'S mill on Reedy Creek. By Jury on condition cut six inches off the top of his Mill Dam or to the place marked by an orge hole and notch cut in the top log. Signed: JOSIAH CARTER, BAYNES CARTER. Wit: JAMES BAKER.

Page 110. 23 November 1780. Suit brought by PETER COPLAND against WATERS DUNN continued to next October Court 1781. Signed: PETER COPLAND; WATERS DUNN. Wit: JACOB COHAN.

Page 111. 28 December 1780. WILLIAM MULLINGS of the county of Henry to EUSEBEOUS STONE for the sum of eighty pounds sells and conveys 150 acres of land more or less, it being the lower part of a tract of land granted WILLIAM MULLINGS 1 March 1773 on both sides of the east fork of Town Creek being the land on which Stone now lives. Signed: WILLIAM (X) MULLINGS.

Pages 112, 113. 13 November 1780. THOMAS RAY of the county of Henry to WILLIAM MULLINGS for the sum of fifteen pounds sells 70 acres of land, it being the upper part of the land granted to WILLIAM

MULLINGS by patent 1 March 1773 on both sides of Town Creek, beginning at a dividing line between RAY and MULLINGS, it being the land RAY now lives on. Signed: THOMAS RAY. Wit: JOHN HUNTER, THOMAS (X) ROBERTS, EDGCOME GUILLIAMS.

Page 113. Power of Attorney. JOHN FREDERICK MILLER of the county of Halifax hereby vested to JAMES SHELTON of Henry County full power of attorney to transact business in land, to convey titles, etc. whereas I have a certain matter in dispute which is a suit in Chancery in General Court brought by WADE'S executors against me for a tract of land now in possession of JOHN MARR. Signed: JOHN F. MILLER. Wit: JOHN DILLARD, WILLIAM SHELTON, JOHN BENDER.

Page 114. 30 August 1780. WILLIAM STEGALL of the county of Halifax to WILLIAM JINKINS of Henry County for the sum of six hundred pounds sells a tract or parcel of land in Henry County containing 190 acres more or less on both sides of Turkey Creek. Signed: WILLIAM (X) STEGALL. Wit: FREDERICK RIVES, JOHN JINKINS, BURWELL RIVES, ALEXANDER RIVES.

Pages 115, 116. 11 December 1780. JOHN MARR and THOMAS BEDFORD of Henry County to GEORGE HAIRSTON for the sum of thirty thousand pounds sell and release all their proportionably part of that dividend tract or parcel of land situated and being in Henry County on the north side of Smith River called and known as the Horseshoe containing by estimate 260 acres more or less, which said parcel of land was conveyed unto said MARR and BEDFORD and GEORGE HAIRSTON by EDMUND LYNE, Esq. by a deed recorded in the county of Henry, the deed conveyed to LYNE from THOMAS MANN RANDOLPH by deed recorded in General Court. Signed: JOHN MARR, THOMAS BEDFORD, JUNR. Wit: PETER HAIRSTON, MORDECAI HORDE, CHRISTOPHER OWENS.

Pages 117, 118. 22 March 1781. JOHN SALMON to THOMAS CREWS for the sum of thirty six pounds sells a tract of land on the waters of Marrowbone Creek, containing 81 acres joins HARMON'S order line. Signed: JOHN SALMON.

Page 118. 26 April 1781. ROBERT WOODS of Henry County to HUGH MARTIN for and in consideration of one ear of Indian Corn, but more especially for great regard and tender love I have unto the said MARTIN I convey a parcel of land in Henry County it being the tract whereon MARTIN is now living containing 222 acres on Chestnut Creek. Signed: ROBERT WOODS. Wit: JOHN DICKERSON, WILLIAM WOODS, JOHN (X) JOHNSTON.

Pages 120, 121. 3 March 1781. WILLIAM FRENCH of Henry County to MICAL CLORE for the sum of thirty pounds conveys and sells land containing 70 acres more or less on the north side of Mayo River, it being part of a tract said FRENCH purchased of THOMAS MANN RANDOLPH. Beginning at HAMON CRITZ line on the bank of the north side of the Mayo River. Signed: WILLIAM FRENCH. Wit: SAMUEL WALKER, ANTHONY SMITH, JESSE WITT.

Pages 121, 122. 26 April 1781. ROBERT JONES, JR. of Henry County, attorney for JOHN MURPHEY to JAMES GREER of Henry County for the sum of one thousand pounds sells land on the waters of Pigg River near the main mountain, containing 336 acres. Land by patent was granted JOHN MURPHEY the 11 December 1780. Signed: ROBERT JONES.

Pages 123, 124. 20 May 1780. BENJAMIN NEAL of the county of Henry to GEORGE BRITTAIN for the sum of one hundred pounds conveys and sells 155 acres on Home Creek joins GILLUMS new line. Signed: BENJAMIN NEAL. Wit: DAVID HARRIS, JOSEPH (X) HARRIS, THOMAS (X) STEPHENS.

Pages 124, 125. 20 March 1781. THOMAS MILLER of Henry County to JOEL WALKER for the sum of one hundred twenty pounds conveys land and tenement lying and being in Henry County 277 acres more or less. Signed: THOMAS MILLER. . .ELIZABETH MILLER, wife of THOMAS relinquishes right of dower.

Pages 126, 127. 3 March 1781. WILLIAM FRENCH of Henry County to WILLIAM CORNWELL of the same for the sum of thirty pounds sells land 300 acres on the south side of Mill Creek, it being part of a tract the said FRENCH purchased of THOMAS MANN RANDOLPH. Beginning on HAMON CRITZ line on the bank of the south side of Mill Creek to Mayo River. Signed: WILLIAM FRENCH. Wit: ANTHONY SMITH, JESSE WITT, SAMUEL WALKER.

Page 128. Lease. I, JOSIAH SMITH of the county of Henry for divers good causes and more especially for the natural affection I have for my son-in-law JACOB STALLINGS do lett and lease to said STALLINGS part of the tract I now live on beginning at where my line corners on JOHN DILLARD'S line, to my first purchase of JAMES SHELTON. To enjoy said property until 1 January 1792. Signed: JOSIAH SMITH. Wit: JOSEPH MORRIS, JOHN DILLARD, JOHN COX, JOHN STAPLES.

Page 129. Power of Attorney. I, JOHN MURPHY of Washington County, North Carolina have made, ordained, constitued and appointed my trusty friend ROBERT JONES, JR. lawful attorney to make lawful rite for a certain tract of land I sold JAMES GREER on the north fork of Pigg River. Signed: JOHN MURPHY. Wit: ISAAC BARTON, JAMES JONES, JOHN RENTFRO, JOSHUA RENTFRO.

Page 130. 26 April 1781. RICHARD MURRELL and MARY his wife of Henry County to RICHARD PILSON of Henry County for the sum of one hundred twenty pounds sells and conveys land on the north side of Irvin (Smith) River it being 71 acres more or less. Lines: CHARLES WITT'S old patent line to THOMAS HOFF'S line. Signed: RICHARD MURRELL. . .MARY, wife of RICHARD MURRELL relinquishes right of dower.

Pages 131, 132. 3 March 1781. WILLIAM FRENCH of the county of Henry to JOSIAH SMITH for the sum of two thousand six hundred pounds sells and conveys land containing by estimate 150 acres on the south side of Mayo River, joins lines of HAMON CRITZ, it being part of a tract purchased of THOMAS RANDOLPH to Mill Creek. Signed: WILLIAM FRENCH. Wit: ANTHONY SMITH, SAMUEL WALKER, JESSE WITT.

Page 133. 12 February 1781. Dower right. The Commonwealth of Virginia to JOHN SALMON, HENRY LYNE and JOHN FONTAINE greetings, whereas WILLIAM SWANSON, SR. by certain indenture hath conveyed unto PHILEMON SOUTHERLAND 150 acres on Bull Runn and as MARY SWANSON cannot travel conveniently to the Courthouse, she hereby relinquishes her right of dower to same.

Pages 134, 135. 26 July 1781. GEORGE TAYLOR to MILES JENNINGS both of Henry County for the sum of five hundred pounds sells 135 acres of land, it being part of the said GEORGE TAYLOR tract. Lines: BRADLEY SMITH and JENNINGS. Signed: GEORGE TAYLOR

Pages 136, 137. 18 July 1781. MILES JENNINGS of the county of Henry to JOHN NICHOLAS of the same for the sum of one thousand pounds sells and conveys 150 acres of land, it being part of the lands of MILES JENNINGS. Beginning at a chestnut tree in RANDOLPH'S order line. Signed: MILES JENNINGS. Wit: JAMES SHELTON, GEORGE TAYLOR, JAMES EAST.

Pages 138, 139.   18 July 1781.   MILES JENNINGS of Henry County to TABITHA DEPRIEST of the same for the sum of one thousand pounds sells 250 acres of land, it being part of the MILES JENNINGS tract, beginning at JOHN NICHOLAS corner post in RANDOLPH'S order line to a hickory on Jack's Branch. Signed: MILES JENNINGS. Wit: JAMES EAST, GEORGE TAYLOR, JAMES SHELTON.

Pages 140, 141.   23 March 1781.   Bill of Sale.   JOHN EARLY of the county of Henry to JAMES CALLAWAY of the county of Bedford, whereas JEREMIAH EARLY late deceased of Bedford County was in his lifetime seized and possessed of one moiety of an estate called WASHINGTON IRON WORKS being in Henry County containing certain lands, tenements and hereditaments as co-partner with said CALLAWAY also of certain slaves, stock of horses, hoggs, cattle, wagon, gears, plantation utensils, blacksmith and carpenters tools and all kind of appartous necessary for carrying on and erecting a sett of iron works. Did make his last will and testament in writing 29 June 1779 wherein said JEREMIAH EARLY devised all that part of his estate which he held in partnership with JAMES CALLAWAY called the WASHINGTON IRON WORKS to his three sons JOSEPH EARLY, JOHN EARLY and JUBAL EARLY recorded in Bedford County. JOHN EARLY for and in consideration of the negros LEWIS, HANNAH, BACCUS, RUTH, CATUS, BECK, PHILLIS, SAM, EDY and LITTLE PHILLIS together with 1/5th part of the negros and their increase which said JAMES is entitled to in right of his wife after the death of MARY EARLY widow and relict of said JEREMIAH EARLY and paid in horses or cattle at the accustom price in the year DCCLXXIV and for a certain quantity of inspected tobacco at the Falls of the James River to the amount of one thousand one hundred seventy five pounds current money off said tobacco to be estimated at 9 pounds and 100 weight and for further consideration of said JAMES CALLAWAY paying for the said JOHN EARLY to the guardians of FRANCIS POLLARD'S children the sum of seven thousand four hundred and two pounds. The said JOHN EARLY hath sold to the said JAMES CALLAWAY 1/3rd of the moiety of the estate called WASHINGTON IRON WORKS. Signed: JOHN EARLY. Wit: THOMAS ARTHUR, JOHN DOIGHTER, JEREMIAH EARLY, STEPHEN SMITH, BARTLETT WADE.

Page 142. 23 August 1781. Deed of Gift. JOHN DANIEL, SR. of the county of Henry do out of love and free goodwill give and forever defend unto my daughter, MARY DANIEL all my house creatures, cattle, hoggs and best feather bed and five hundred pounds cash after my decease and the decease of her mother SARAH DANIEL. Signed: JOHN (X) DANIELS. Wit: EDWARD TATUM, MARTHA (X) TATUM.

Page 143. 3 January 1780. Deed of Gift. THOMAS HARN of South Carolina for and in consideration of the love and good will and affection which I have towards my loving brother HENRY HARN of South Carolina have given and granted unto the said HENRY HARN all my property at my decease. Recorded 23 August 1781. Signed: THOMAS HARN. Wit: WILLIAM WEST, SIMON FRAZER, EDIETH HARN.

Pages 144, 145. 24 September 1781. ARCHELAUS HUGHES of the county of Henry to AUGUSTINE THOMAS sells for the sum of twenty five pounds land in Henry County being 239 acres on the north fork of Mayo River bounded by GRAY'S corner. Signed: A. HUGHES. Wit: ANTHONY SMITH, JAMES FULKERSON, MILES JENINGS.

Pages 145, 146. 3 September 1781. ELIZABETH WEBB executrix and MERRY WEBB executor of the last will and testament of MERRY WEBB, deceased to PHILIP RYAN, ELIZABETH WEBB and MERRY WEBB for the sum of two thousand six hundred eighty pounds sell land in Henry County on the north side of Irvin River containing by estimate 150 acres. Signed: ELIZABETH (X) WEBB, MERRY (X) WEBB. Wit: H. SANSON, RICHARD WILSON, JOHN HALL, JOHN (X) BURGIS.

Pages 147, 148. 3 September 1781. ELIZABETH WEBB and MERRY WEBB executors of MERRY WEBB, deceased to JOHN REA. Witness that PHILIP RYAN for and in consideration of one thousand eight hundred pounds by the said JOHN REA paid for land lying between Irvin River and Marriabone Creek, being 54 acres joining JOHN RICE. Signed: ELIZABETH (X) WEBB, MERRY (X) WEBB. Wit: ... SWANSON, RICHARD WILSON, JOHN (X) BURGIS, PHIL RYAN.

Pages 149, 150. 19 November 1781. ANDREW FARGUSON of Botetourt County to JOHN FARGUSON of Henry County for the sum of eighteen pounds conveys land in Henry County on both sides of Story Creek, beginning at an oak in WILLIAM MCDANIEL'S line being

98 acres. Signed: ANDREW (X) FARGUSON. . .CATHERON, wife of ANDREW FARGUSON relinquishes her right of dower.

Pages 150, 151. 6 August 1781. MICHAEL ROWLAND of the county of Henry to BAYNES CARTER of the same for the sum of one thousand pounds sells and conveys a tract or parcel of land in Henry County on both sides of Reed Creek it being 121 acres more or less beginning on the south side of Reedy Creek. .to RANDOLPH'S line. Signed: MICHAEL ROWLAND. Wit: JOHN COX, JULIUS SCRUGGS, JUNAH (X) MEREDITH.

Pages 152, 153. 24 May 1781. STEPHEN LEE of Henry County to SHADRACK WOODSON for the sum of three thousand one hundred pounds sells one parcel of land it being 160 acres more or less and being on the branch of Blackwater River called Rich Run. Signed: STEPHEN LEE. Wit: ISAAC BATES, JOSEPH MCCANN, JESSE (X) WHITE, SHOWERS PRICE, WILLIAM BELL.

Pages 154, 155. 22 November 1782. MORDECAI HOARD of the Parish of Henry and county of Henry to GEORGE WALLER for the sum of one hundred fifty two pounds conveys all that part of a tract, part or parcel of land in Henry County containing 140 acres more or less and being part of a tract of 1,750 acres purchased of MARTIN KEY, attorney in fact for WALTER KING of the Kingdom of Great Britian that deed recorded in Henry County in 1780. The 140 acres beginning at the mouth of Jordon's Creek, a branch of Smith River, thence up Smith River as it meanders to the mouth of School branch below the Narrows, thence up the said branch to RANDOLPH'S line. Signed: MORDECAI HORD.

Pages 155, 156. 4 July 1781. MICHAEL DILLINGHAM of the county of Henry and parish of Patrick to SAMUEL BYRD of the same for the sum of one hundred pounds conveys land and all on it on Reed Creek. Signed: MICHAEL (X) DILLINGHAM. Wit: JOHN BARKSDILL, JESSE HEARD, CHRISTOPHER OWENS, JOHN COX.

Pages 157, 158. 9 October 1780. JAMES COX, SENR. of Henry County to THOMAS EARLS of the same for the sum of fifteen pounds grant, bargain and sell one parcel of land being 50 acres more or less bounded by the boundary hereof WILLIAM TUNSTALL and JAMES COX, JR. Signed: JAMES COX, SR. Wit: THOMPSON DICKERSON, JAMES COX, JOHN DICKERSON.

Pages 158, 159. 4 October 1781. JOHN CONNAWAY of the county of Henry to ROBERT PEREGO of the same. That JOHN CONNAWAY and MARY CONNAWAY, his mother, for the sum of five pounds sells unto the said PEREGO a parcel of land containing 35 acres more or less on the branches of Leatherwood Creek beginning in WYATT'S line. Signed: JOHN CONNAWAY, MARY CONNAWAY. Wit: ROBERT (X) WATSON, ASIAS (X) GALIHORN.

Page 160. Bond. Bond of ROBERT HAIRSTON as he is constituted and appointed Sherif of Henry County by his Excellency the Governor. Signed: Bondsmen: ROBERT HAIRSTON, WILL. TUNSTALL, JOHN SALMON, HENRY LYNE, GEORGE HAIRSTON.

Pages 161, 162. 6 September 1781. RICHARD PARSLEY of the county of Henry and his wife NANCY to ROBERT PEREGO of the same for the sum of fifteen pounds sells and conveys 100 acres of land more or less in the county of Henry on the branches of Beaver Creek beginning at a chestnut on the south side of PARSLEY'S ridge path on the old line...to WALKER'S order line. Signed: RICHARD (X) PARSLEY, NANCY (X) PARSLEY. Wit: ROBERT (X) WATSON, JOSEPH PEREGO (X), SAMUEL WATSON.

Pages 162, 163. 11 September 1781. RICHARD PARSLEY and NANCY his wife of Henry County to ROBERT WATSON for the sum of fifteen pounds conveys land containing 50 acres more or less on the branches of Beaver Creek, joins ROBERT PEDIGO'S corner. Signed: RICHARD (X) PARSLEY, ANN (X) PARLSLEY (?). Wit: JOHN BRISCOE, ROBERT (X) PEDIGO, SAMUEL WATSON, JOSEPH PEDIGO.

Pages 164, 165. 30 September 1781. RICHARD PARSLEY and ANN his wife to SAMUEL WATSON for the sum of fifteen pounds sells and conveys a parcel of land containing 50 acres on the branches of Beaver Creek, beginning at ROBERT WATSON'S corner. Signed: RICHARD (X) PARSLEY, ANN (X) PARSLEY. Wit: JOHN CONNAWAY, WILLIAM ACUFF, JOSEPH PEDIGOE, ROBERT WATSON.

Pages 165, 166. 4 August 1781. JOHN MULLINGS of the county of Henry to STEPHEN STONE of the same in consideration of twenty five pounds old trade sells and conveys land containing 70 acres more or less on the east fork of Town Creek, beginning at EUSEBEOUS STONE'S upper line, following the old line mentioned in WILLIAM MULLINGS pattent thence to a dividing line made for THOMAS HILL. Signed: JOHN (X) MULLINGS. Wit: JOHN HUNTER, WILLIAM HUNTER, EUSEBEOUS STONE.

Page 167. 23 January 1782. ELISHA ESTES of Henry County to JOEL ESTES of the same in consideration of the sum of one hundred pounds sells and conveys land on both sides of Snow Creek containing 220 acres it being the plantation that ELISHA ESTES now lives on and bounded by the lines of TULLY CHOICE, SAMUEL PATTERSON and JAMES BARBERYES land. Signed: ELISHA ESTES. Wit: WILLIAM RYAN, BENJAMIN COOK, BENJAMIN HOLMES. . .MEMORANDUM: That the said ESTES his heirs and etc. is not to have the said tract of land till after the death of the said ESTES and his wife MARY. This memo made before signed.

Pages 168, 169, 170. 26 February 1782. THOMAS EDWARDS of Henry County to DORROTHY MINIS (MINNIS) the widow of JOHN MINIS deceased of the same county for the sum of one hundred pounds sells land on the draughts of Tolct (?) Creek beginning at WILLIAM EDWARDS corner hickory and containing 157 acres more or less. Signed: THOMAS EDWARDS.

Pages 170, 171, 172. 26 February 1782. THOMAS EDWARDS of Henry County to JAMES EDWARDS of the same sells land on the Draughts of TOECLOUT (?) Creek, beginning at the Widow MINIS' corner and lines of WILLIAM JAMES and WILLIAM EDWARDS containing 157 acres more or less. Signed: THOMAS EDWARDS.

Pages 172, 173. 28 February 1782. MARVELL NASH to WILLIAM LOVELL both of the county of Henry sells and conveys land on both sides of Beaver Creek for the sum of seventy five pounds, it being 1,000 acres more or less adjoining THOMAS COOPER and JOSEPH COOPER. Signed: MARVEL NASH.

Page 174. 27 September 1781. JOHN LAW, SR. of the county of Henry to JESSE LAW of the same for the sum of fifty pounds sells and conveys land on Simmon's Creek it being 600 acres more or less. . . crosses Jack's Creek. Signed: JOHN (X) LAW. Wit: RICHARD PERRYMAN, BENONA PERYMAN, JOHN SWANSON, JESSE HEARD, RICHARD EDMONDSON.

Pages 175, 176. 14 February 1782. Agreement. RACHEL GOUGE of the county of Henry of the one part and PATRICK HENRY and JOHN MARR of the other part for in consideration of the sum of five shillings sell one stallion colt, a sorrel, one grey gelding, one black mare, twelve head of nett cattle old and young marked with cross and slit in the right ear and hole in the left, 50 head hogs young and old of the same mark, and 21 head of sheep, 2 beds and furniture, 6 pewter plates, 1 dish, 1 dutch oven and large iron pott. To have and hold the said stock, etc. to the said PATRICK HENRY and JOHN MARR to the following intents and purposes and trust viz: That the said RACHEL GOUGE during her life whether sole or married to use, occupy and enjoy the same to and for her sole and separate use and benefit and not subject to any future husbands use or control and after her death to and for the absolute use and benefit of all the children of the said RACHEL GOUGE now living equally divided as to make the shares of MARY RICE, NATHAN GOUGE, JANE GOUGE which they have already received from the said RACHEL GOUGE equal with their brothers and sisters. Signed: RACHEL (X) GOUGE, P. HENRY, JOHN MARR.

Pages 177, 178. 29 March 1781. PHILIP HUTCHERSON to WILLIAM LONG both of Henry County sells and conveys for the sum of twenty pounds land containing 274 acres by survey on Burch Branch of Snow Creek with lines of WILLIAM HEARD and THOMAS PRUNTY. Signed: PHILIP (X) HUTCHERSON. Wit: SPENCER CLACK, BENJAMIN CHANDLER, BENJAMIN HOMS. . .PRUDENCE HUTCHERSON relinquishes right of dower.

Page ?. 29 March 1782. Bond. Bond of ABRAHAM PENN to serve the office of Coroner of the County of Henry.

Pages 179, 180. 29 March 1782. Bond. Bond of JOHN SALMON to serve as Commissioner for collecting certain taxes agreeable to an act passed at the last session of Assembly...a tax for certain enumerated commodities.

Page 180. 28 March 1782. Bond. Bond of ARCHLAUS HUGHES who is appointed as one of the Commissioners for the county of Henry.

Pages 181, 182. MARY RAMSEY and GEORGE RAMSEY administrators with the Will annexed of JOHN RAMSEY, deceased of Henry County to JEREMIAH EARLY also of Henry County. For the sum of thirty five pounds MARY RAMSEY and GEORGE RAMSEY sell and convey a certain parcel of land on the branches of

Chestnut Creek containing 240 acres more or less, being part of 346 acres granted said JOHN RAMSEY, deceased, by patent bearing date at Williamsburg 20 October 1779. Signed: MARY (X) RAMSEY, GEORGE (X) RAMSEY. Wit: JOHN COX, JOHN RENTFRO, PETER SAUNDERS, JESSE HEARD.

Pages 183, 184. 20 October 1781. ISAAC JONES and RACHEL his wife to JOSEPH LEWIS for the sum of eighty pounds convey and sell land containing 195 acres it being part of a tract on both sides of the north fork of Pigg River by patent bearing date at Williamsburgh 20 July 1768, joins PETER YOUNG'S line. Signed: ISAAC JONES. Wit: PETER YOUNG, ISAAC JANNEY, JACOB OLDAKERS, ROBERT JONES.

Pages 185, 186. 25 April 1782. ROBERT JONES of the county of Henry to GEORGE HALE of the county of Louden for the sum of twenty pounds conveys land on a fork of Pigg River containing 100 acres adjoining lines of ROBERT JONES. Signed: ROBERT JONES. Wit: JESSE HEARD, PETER YOUNG, JOHN WILLS.

Pages 187, 188, <u>199</u>. 22 April 1782. DARBY RYAN of the county of Henry to WILLIAM STANDEFER for the sum of two hundred pounds conveys 370 acres of land by survey bearing date of 30 April 1779 on the branches of Pigg River. Lines: HARVEY JONES, ROBERT JONES, THOMAS JONES and HENRY JONES. Signed: DARBY RYAN. Wit: MARK RENTFROE, THOMAS NUNN, JOHN COX, ELIJAH JONES, JOHN SALMON, R. WILLIAMS.

Pages 189 thru 198 are skipped.

Pages 199, 200. Bond. Bond of ROBERT MASON of the county of Henry is appointed a Commissioner of same.

Pages 200, 201. 3 November 1781. LEWIS MORGAN and his wife CHRISTIAN and THOMAS MORGAIN and his wife (?) both of the state of North Carolina and county of Washington for the sum of two hundred fifty pounds sell and convey unto SAMUEL PATTERSON a certain parcel or tract of land being the plantation the said LEWIS MORGAN formerly lived on near the ford and mouth of Chestnut Creek bounded by ISHAM HODGES on the upper and a survey the said LEWIS MORGAN made himself on the said Chestnut Creek containing 150 acres more or less. Signed: LEWIS MORGAIN, CHRISTIAN MORGAIN, THOMAS MORGAIN, SAREY MORGAIN. Wit: TULLY CHOICE, SAMUEL BOLLING, JESSE KERBY, WILLIAM CHOICE.

Note: 26 March 1782 - SAREY MORGAIN listed as MARY MORGAIN in the Clerk's recording.

Pages 202, 203. 24 April 1782. WILLIAM RYAN of the county of Henry to CHRISTOPHER SKILMON of the same county for the sum of sixty pounds sells a parcel of land on a branch of Snow Creek containing 200 acres more or less. Signed: WILLIAM RYAN. Wit: HENRY (X) BARKSDALE, JOEL ESTES.

Pages 203, 204, 205. 28 September 1781. CHARLES FOSTER and ANN his wife to HENRY SUMPTER all being of Henry County sell for the sum of one hundred fifty pounds land being 50 acres on both sides Smith River. Signed: CHARLES FOSTER, ANNE FOSTER. Wit: RALPH MITCHELL, EDWARD (X) BAKER, WILLIAM MARTIN.

Pages 206, 207. 15 April 1782. THOMAS JONES of Henry County to WILLIAM MAVITY of the same sells for the sum of five pounds a parcel of land containing 6 acres more or less, it being part of the tract which said JONES has on both sides of the Island Run on a branch of Pigg River adjoining MAVITY'S own line. Signed: THOMAS JONES. Wit: WILLIAM STANDEFER, WILLIAM DUNN, ROBERT PUSEY, JOHN COX, JOHN DILLARD, JOSEPH LEWIS.

Pages 208, 209. 23 April 1782. THOMAS STOCKTON of the county of Henry to JAMES BARTLETT of the same for the sum of one hundred twenty pounds sells all that tract of land situated in Henry County on both sides of the north fork of the Mayo River, containing by estimate 94 acres. Signed: THOMAS STOCKTON. Wit: BALDWIN ROWLAND, JOHN BARKSDALE, BRICE MARTIN. . .MARY STOCKTON, wife of THOMAS STOCKTON releases her right of dower.

Pages 211, 212. 23 ..... 1782. WILLIAM LOVELL of the county of Henry to MICKEL DILLINGHAM of the same for the sum of sixty pounds sells and conveys a tract of land lying on Reedy Creek containing 190 acres more or less, beginning at ARIS VAUGN'S line on the south side of Reedy Creek to WILLIAM HEARD'S line. Signed: WILLIAM LOVELL. Wit: JONATHAN HANES, RHODON RADMUN, ARIS (X) VAUGN.

Page ?. 25 December 1770. Transfer of Title. MARK FOSTER of the county of Pittsylvania and province of Virginia, School Master and MARY FOSTER his wife convey to CHARLES FOSTER, his son. That the said MARY FOSTER, his wife, during her widowhood by the name of MARY HOFF obtained a warrant the Honourable the Propriateries bearing date ___ of ___ in the year 17__, for a certain tract of land situated in New Berrey township in the county of York and province of Pennsylvania upon the waters of Yealow Bretches adjoining the land of WILLIAM PACKWOOD and THOMAS CAMBLE containing 100 acres. MARK FOSTER and his wife MARY for the sum of five shillings grant, sell unto the said CHARLES FOSTER the said land, he paying the remainder of purchase money, interest and quit rente thereon due to the Chief Lord or Lords. Signed: MARK FOSTER, MARY (X) FOSTER. Wit: WILLIAM JONES, SAMUEL PACKWOOD.

Pages 215, 216. 23 May 1782. THOMAS HALE and JANE his wife of the county of Henry to JAMES TURNER of the same, for the sum of one hundred fifty pounds sell and convey a parcel of land containing 297 acres on both sides of Pigg River...joins THOMAS JONES' old line and MAVITY'S. Signed: THOMAS HALE, JEANE HALE.

Pages 217, 218. 27 May 1782. MALACHI CUMMINGS of Henry County to JACOB ADAMS of Henry County for the sum of fifty four pounds ten shillings sells one tract of land it being in the county of Fauquire containing 250 acres it being part of 926 acres formerly the property of THOMAS BERRY, deceased. Signed: MALACHI (X) CUMMINGS. Wit: JACOB ADAMS.

Page 219. 24 May 1782. AMBROSE HOLD being firmly bound unto ELISHA RICHARD and JOEL ESTES in the sum of ten thousand pounds. The condition is such that the above bound AMBROSE HOLT him nor his heirs is never at no time to lay any claim against the estate of ELISHA ESTES, deceased, nor put up any claim to a negroe woman slave named NANN. Signed: AMBROSE (X) HOLT. Wit: GEORGE HAIRSTON, JOHN COX.

Page 220. Bond. Bond of ROBERT HAIRSTON in the amount of ten thousand pounds that he shall collect taxes as imposed by an Act of the Assembly. Signed: Bondsmen: ROBERT HAIRSTON, A. HUGHES, GEORGE HAIRSTON, P. HAIRSTON, JOHN MARR.

Pages 221, 222. 14 March 1782. JOHN MANNIN and JOHN SIMMONS of Henry County to JOHN HARDMAN of the same for the sum of fifty pounds the said MANNIN and SIMMONS sell and convey a parcel of land being 100 acres more or less beginning at a corner in ARCHABLE ROBERTSON'S line. Signed: JOHN MANNIN, JOHN (X) SIMMONS. Wit: LEMUEL LANIER, DANIEL FAD (FORD), CHARLES HARDMAN. . .SUSANNAH MANNIN, wife of JOHN MANNIN releases right of dower.

Page 223. 15 June 1782. Deed of Gift. JOHN HARDMAN of the county of Henry to DANIEL FORD and MARY FORD, datter (daughter) of said JOHN HARDMAN, for and in consideration of the natural love and affection which he hath unto the said DANIEL FORD and MARY FORD his wife give 50 acres of land beginning at a corner of JESSE WILLINGHAM on Marrowbone Creek, JOHN RICHARDSON'S line. After the death of DANIEL FORD the land to go to his son DAVID FORD. Signed: JOHN (X) HARDMAN.

Pages 224, 225. 29 December 1781. GEORGE REEVES of the county of Henry to GEORGE SUMPTER of the county of Charlotte for the sum of twenty pounds sells a parcel of land containing 106 acres beginning at DAVID CHADWELL'S corner on the south side of Smith River. Signed: GEORGE REEVES. Wit: HENRY SUMPTER, AGGE SUMPTER, ADMUND SUMTER.

Pages 226, 227. 23 July 1782. GEORGE HAIRSTON of the county of Henry to JOHN SNEED for the sum of one hundred pounds sells and conveys 200 acres more or less on both sides of Joincrack Creek, it being the lower tract of the tract of land that SILAS RATLIF now lives on beginning at an oak, the line that ROBERT JONES' executors of DANIEL RYAN Estate run between WILLIAM RATLIF and DARBY RYAN and JAMES EDWARDS line, BENJAMIN HUBBARD and WARDS line. Signed: GEORGE HAIRSTON.

Pages 227, 228, 229. 22 April 1782. EDWARD RICHARD of the county of Henry to SHADRICK RICHARDS for the sum of one hundred pounds sells all mesuage or tenaments, land, being 250 acres, on both sides of the north fork of Chestnut Creek. Signed: EDWARD RICHARD. . .ELIZABETH RICHARDS, wife of EDWARD RICHARD, releases right of dower.

Pages 229, 230. 25 July 1782. JERIAH HOLCOMB, administrator of GRYMES HOLCOMB, deceased of Henry County sells to MICHAEL ROWLAND for the sum of one hundred pounds land on the waters of Town Creek and Chestnut Creek, it being 554 acres more or less which was granted GRYMES HOLCOMB by patent dated at Richmond. Signed: JEREIAH (X) HOLCOMB.

Pages 231, 232. 18 May 1782. DARBY RYAN and MARY

his wife of Henry County to JAMES TURNER for the sum of three pounds sell land on both sides of Pig River it being 52 acres more or less, beginning at DARBY RYAN'S corner, MILLER DOGET'S line and crosses Pig River. Signed: DARBY RYAN. Wit: THOMAS HALE, THOMAS PRUNTY, PETER SAUNDERS.

Pages 233, 234. 5 April 1782. JAMES STANDEFER of Henry County to BAILEY CARTER sells land on the waters of Outer Creek in the amount of 400 acres, joins PETER SAUNDER'S line. Signed: JAMES STANDEFER. Wit: DANIEL ROSS, WILLIAM MAVITY, EDGECOMB WILLIAMS, NATHANIEL DICKSON, THOMAS HILL, LEWIS DEWASE.

Pages 235, 236. 1 April 1782. ABRAHAM PENN and RUTH his wife of the county of Henry to WILLIAM WHITSETT of said county for the sum of five hundred pounds sells and conveys land on both sides of Little Beaver Creek (alias Red Bank Creek) containing by estimate 1,350 acres joining the lines of: JOHN COOPER, THOMAS COOPER, ROBERT STOCKTON and PETER COPLAND. Signed: ABRAHAM PENN, RUTH PENN. Wit: JOHN COX, JOHN STAPLES, WILLIAM (X) LYNCH.

Pages 236, 237, 238. 25 July 1782. JOHN NEVILS of the county of Henry to RICHARD KERBY of the said county for the sum of thirty pounds sells and conveys land on Sycamore Creek containing 334 acres more or less with the lines of: THOMAS MORRISON, LUKE FOLEY and WARD. Signed: JOHN NEVILS. Wit: none. . .SARAH NEVILS, wife of JOHN release right of dower.

Pages 239, 240. 30 September 1782. WALTER KING COLE of the county of Henry to JOHN ROWLAND of the said county for the sum of fifteen pounds sells and conveys a certain tract of land containing by patent 75 acres more or less on the south side of Smith River being a corner of Cole's Marrowbone tract joining the lines of: JAMES MEREDITH, BRICE MARTIN and JOHN ALEXANDER. Signed: WALTER KING COLE.

Pages 240, 241, 242. 22 January 1782. RICHARD MCCOY of the county of Montgomery to ANDREW KELLY of Henry County sells for the sum of fifty pounds a parcel of land situated in Henry County containing 100 acres on the branches of Blackwater River. Signed: RICHARD MCCOY. Wit: ... DUNN, STEPHEN LEE, SHADRICK WOODSON, JOHN (X) RETTER, JOHN BLAIN, JOSHUA (X) RENTFRO.

Pages 242, 243, 244. 22 January 1782. RICHARD MCCOY of the county of Montgomery to ANDREW KELLY of the county of Henry sells for the sum of seventy pounds a tract of land containing more or less 137 acres on the branches of Blackwater River. Signed: RICHARD MCCOY. Wit: same as previous deed.

Pages 244, 245. 22 January 1782. RICHARD MCCOY of the county of Montgomery to ABRAHAM RITTER of the county of Henry sells for the sum of sixty pounds 137 acres more or less on Blackwater River branches. Signed: RICHARD MCCOY. Wit: same as page 242.

Page 246. 23 August 1782. Inquisition. Held by ABRAHAM PENN, Excheator for the county of Henry at the premises on Smith River by oath of GEORGE WALLER, foreman, JOHN SALMON, ALEXANDER HUNTER, JOHN BARKSDALE, JOSIAH CARTER, ANTHONY BITTEN, JOHN STOKES, THOMAS COOPER, JOHN COOPER, JOSEPH KING, IGNACUS SIMS and JAMES BARBERRY. Whereas, a tract of land (450 acres) belonging to JAMES and ROBERT DONALD & Company, Merchants and partners of Great Brittian and are British subjects and ought to vest in the Commonwealth, according to an Act of Assembly.

Pages 247, 248. 22 August 1782. JOHN ACUFF of the county of Henry to WILLIAM COCKRAM of said county sells and conveys for the sum of one hundred twenty six pounds land on Leatherwood Creek which joins BOLING'S line. Signed: JOHN ACUFF.

Pages 248, 249. JOHN WELLS of the county of Henry to JOHN HAILEY of the same county for the sum of twenty pounds conveys land containing 297 acres on the south branches of Leatherwood Creek beginning at Lomax & Company's corner, JACOB RIGIOR'S line, WILLIAM BROWN'S line. Signed: JOHN WELLS.

Pages 250, 251. 15 September 1782. EDWARD SMITH of Henry County to JOHN SHEALDS for the sum of four hundred pounds conveys land on Turacock Creek more or less 400 acres beginning at JOHN CUN-NINGHAM'S corner. Signed: EDWARD SMITH.

Pages 251, 252. 22 August 1782. HUGH INNES of Henry County to JAMES MURPHY for the sum of one hundred pounds sells and conveys land on Daniels Creek being 230 acres more or less, beginning at a red oak in PETER COPLAND'S line. Signed: HUGH INNES.

Pages 253, 254. 22 April 1782. ROBERT HOOKER of the county of Montgomery to BENJAMIN HAWKINS of Henry County for the sum of thirty pounds sells a parcel of land containing 309 acres on the waters of Honens (Home ?) Creek and Hosepater (Horsepasture ?) Creek joining the lands of: WILLIAM TAYLOR, DRURY SALMON, JOHN MARR, JACOB KOGAR and RICHARD WELSH. Signed: ROBERT (X) HOOKER, ELLIS (X) HOOKER. Wit: ISAAC SMITH, WILLIAM TAYLOR, WILLIAM LOWELL, DRURY SALMON.

Page 255. 26 August 1782. JOHN HEARD of Henry County to BENJAMIN DUVALL of said county for the sum of thirty one pounds sells and conveys 330 acres more or less of land lying on the branches of Pig River with the lines of: Mapole Swamp and JOHN ROBERTSON. Signed: JOHN HEARD. Wit: JESSE HEARD, LEWIS DUVALL, STEPHEN HEARD.

Pages 256, 257. 4 September 1782. STEPHEN HEARD of the county of Henry to ISHAM BLANKENSHIP of same for the sum of seventeen pounds sells a tract of land containing 150 acres more or less joining LUMSDAN. Signed: STEPHEN HEARD. Wit: ISREL STANDEFER, JOHN HEARD, HEZEKIAH BLANKENSHIP.

Pages 258, 259. 15 September 1782. Deed of Gift. EDWARD SMITH of the county of Henry to JOHN CUNNINGHAM of the same. SMITH for his real good will and pleasure does give the said CUNNINGHAM one parcel of land on both sides of Turcacock Creek containing 230 acres more or less. Signed: EDWARD SMITH.

Pages 259, 260. 19 October 1782. AMBRUS (AMBROSE) HOLT of the county of Henry to JESSE HALL of said county for the sum of fifty seven pounds ten shillings sells 120 acres of land more or less on the north side of Pigg River. Signed: AMBROSE (X) HOLT.

Pages 261, 262. 21 October 1782. Deed of Gift. JACOB COGER (KOGER) to HENRY COGER for and in consideration of divers good causes and more especially for the natural affection for my son do grant, convey to be the property of my son HENRY after my decease to a certain tract or parcel of land on both sides of Stones Creek being 285 acres. Signed: JACOB (X) KOGER. Wit: PETER COGER, JOHN DILLARD, MARY (X) COGER.

Page 263. 1782. Bill of Sale. JOHN MAKORY (MCCOY) of the county of Henry for the sum of two hundred pounds paid by ANDREW REA sell unto him a negroe man slave by the name of Sampson. Signed: JOHN MACKORY (MCCOYE). Wit: REUBEN PAYNE, NANCY (X) PAYNE.

Page 263. 20 April 1782. I, ANDREW REA, oblige myself and heirs to give up the above bill of sale to the within mentioned JOHN MACKORY if he pays up two bonds which I now hath for two negroes which becomes due 15 July next. Signed: ANDREW REA. Wit: REUBEN PAYNE, NANCY (X) PAYNE.

Pages 264, 265. 24 October 1782. AMBRUS (AMBROSE) HOLT of the county of Henry to PHILMER GREEN for a certain amount of money do convey 80 acres more or less on both sides of Pigg River joining the lines of: WILLIAM CLAY, JESSE HALL, DAVID CERBA (KERBY ?), JOHN DICKENSON and WILLIAM KEEN. Signed: AMBROSE (X) HOLT.

Pages 266, 267. 21 August 1782. DARBY RYAN to the heirs of THOMAS CUMINGS for the sum of one hundred pounds sells and conveys 162 acres on both sides of Oter Creek. Signed: DARBY RYAN. Wit: PETER SAUNDERS, JUDITH SAUNDERS, CON REGAN, MARY SANDERS. . .Receipt says received of THOMAS CUMINGS one hundred pounds.

Pages 268, 269. 24 September 1782. THOMAS CHOWNING of the county of Henry to JOHN KELLEY for the sum of fifty pounds sells and conveys 61 acres of land on the south side of Smith River adjoining WILLIAM SAMS and on Drag Creek. Signed: THOMAS CHOWNING. Wit: SAMPSON (X) MAXEY, HENRY (X) MANNON, FRANCIS (X) KINGTON.

Pages 270, 271. 22 August 1782. JOHN KELLY of the county of Henry to WILLIAM RICE of the same for the sum of ten pounds conveys land on the north side of Smith River containing by estimate 76 acres more or less and joins ELKINS corner. Signed: JOHN KELLEY.

Page 272, 273. 26 September 1782. ARCHIBALD ROBERTSON of the county of Henry to STEPHEN RENO for the sum of thirty pounds sells and conveys 50 acres of land, it being part of a tract granted said ROBERTSON, joins lines of: JOHN SIMMONS and JOHN HARDMAN. Signed: ARCHIBALD ROBERTSON. Wit:

DANIEL FORD, JOHN (X) SIMMONS, WILLIAM (X) FENCH.

Pages 273, 274. 1782. WILLIAM CORNWELL and his wife, _____ of the county of Henry to WILLIAM HAMMITT for the sum of twelve pounds sell land on the south side of the north Mayo River on Mill Creek containing 73 acres more or less. Signed: WILLIAM (X) CORNWELL.

Pages 275, 276. 28 November 1782. Power of Attorney. WILLIAM JAMERSON and FLOREANA JAMISON his wife send greetings. Whereas WILLIAM JAMISON and FLOREANA his wife seized in fee part of a lot in the town of Charleston in the state of Maryland containing one acre more or less as also of part a certain piece of land situated in the county of Cecil state of Maryland being the tract where JOSEPH THOMPSON died without will. The above lot and parcel of land descended to JEAN ARSKINS and said FLOREANA JAMISON daughters of said JOSEPH THOMPSON as co-heiress of said father. WILLIAM JAMISON and FLOREANA JAMISON appoint and impower HENRY ARSKIN of Maryland to lease the said land measuge and lot or sell. Signed: WILLIAM JAMISON, FLOREANA JAMISON. Wit: ARTHUR EDWARDS, SAMUEL RANDOLPH.

Pages 276, 277. 1 August 1782. HELENNER TURBORN of the county of Henry to JESSE WILLINGHAM for the sum of twenty five pounds sells 50 acres of land it being a tract granted HELENNER TURBON by bargain and sale which appears more fully in records of said county, the land being on Marrowbone Creek adjoining land of JOHN HARDMAN. Signed: HELENNER (X) TABORN. Wit: DANIEL FORD, CHARLES HARDMAN, THOMAS HAY.

Pages 278, 279. 28 November 1782. JOSEPH WEBSTER of the county of Henry to AMOS EVANS for the sum of fifteen pounds sells a parcel of land on the south side of Smith River. Signed: JOSEPH WEBSTER.

Pages 280, 281. 28 November 1782. JAMES TAYLOR of the county of Henry to ROBERT HAMPTON for a certain amount of money sells a parcel or tract of land on the fork of Mayo River containing 200 acres more or less. Signed: JAMES TAYLOR.

Pages 281, 282, 283. 24 September 1782. JOHN KELLEY of Henry County to SAMSON MAXEY for the sum of ten pounds sells 150 acres on the north side of the River where SAMSON MAXEY now liveth beginning at Rockhouse Branch and with lines of WILLIAM RICE. Signed: JOHN KELLEY, WINNAFRED (X) KELLEY. Wit: THOMAS CHOWNING, FRANCES (X) KINGTON, HENRY (X) MANNON.

Pages 283, 284. 28 March 1782. THOMAS PRUNTY of the county of Henry to SAMUEL RANDOLPH for the sum of forty pounds sells, grants and conveys 105 acres being part of a tract of 350 acres granted said PRUNTY by patent 12 October 1779. Signed: THOMAS PRUNTY. Wit: ABRAHAM VANDEVENTER, MARY VANDEVENTER, DANIEL JONES.

Page 285. 28 September 1782. Bill of Sale. JOSEPH COOK of Guilford County, North Carolina have this day sold unto DAVID WILLIS of the county of Henry, state of Virginia one negroe boy named Fridy for a valuable consideration. Signed: JOSEPH COOK. Wit: BENJAMIN COOK, SAMUEL BOLLING, WILLIAM (X) DILLINGHAM.

Pages 286, 287. 9 January 1783. CHARLES BURNETT of Henry County and CATHERINE his wife to ROBERT PEREGOY of the same county for the sum of ten pounds sells 52 acres of land on the head of Mulberry Creek. Signed: CHARLES (X) BURNETT, CATHERINE (X) BURNETT. Wit: JOHN GOLEHORN, JOSEPH PERIGOY, ROBERT WATSON, JOHN CONNAWAY.

Pages 287, 288, 289. 20 October 1781. NICKLESS DARNALL and his wife SUSANNA of Henry County to GEORGE MARTIN for the sum of eighty pounds sells and conveys land on both sides of the south fork of Sandy River 204 acres. Signed: NICHOS DARNALL, SUSANNA (X) DARNALL. Wit: THOMAS DICKERSON, THOMPSON DICKERSON, J. ALLSUP, SAMUEL MOSLEY.

Pages 289, 290. 18 January 1783. GEORGE MARTIN and his wife CHARITY of the county of Henry to THOMAS RICHARDSON of the county of Pittsylvania for the sum of eighty five pounds sell, grant and convey a parcel of land containing 204 acres on the south fork of Sandy River. Signed: GEORGE MARTIN, CHARITY MARTIN. Wit: ARTHER NASH, SAMUEL MOSLEY, MOSES TUCK.

Pages 290, 291, 292. 30 October 1782. JOSIAH HODGES of the county of Henry to JAMES COWDEN of the same for the sum of ten pounds sells and conveys land on both sides of Pigg River containing 23 acres more or less, on the south side of said

River near the mouth of a spring branch below a water grist mill belonging to said COWDEN with RICHARD WILTON'S old line. Signed: JOSIAH (X) HODGES. Wit: JOHN DICKERSON, WILLIAM COWDEN, SAMUEL PATTERSON.

Pages 293, 294. 23 February 1783. ROBERT BOLTON of the county of Henry to WILLIAM YOUNG of the county of Pittsylvania for the sum of two hundred pounds sells, grants and conveys a parcel of land containing 1,034 acres on both sides of Snow Creek, beginning at COPLAND'S corner and with lines of RIDLEY YOUNG and ARCHIBALD YOUNG. Signed: ROBERT BOLTON. Wit: ROBERT PERRYMAN.

Pages 295, 296. 27 February 1783. THOMAS WILSON and his wife MARY of the county of Henry and parish of Patrick to WILLIAM PARKS of the same sell for the sum of one hundred pounds land on both sides of Smith River where the said THOMAS WILSON now lives containing 100 acres adjoining lands of PATRICK HENRY, MARTHA WILSON, JACOB STALLINGS and others. Signed: THOMAS (X) WILSON.

Page 296, 297, 298. 7 March 1783. JOHN GRISHAM of the county of Henry to SAMUEL CLARK of the same for the sum of four hundred pounds sells and conveys a parcel of land containing 744 acres on Spoon Creek in two different surveys, joins land of JOHN MARR. Signed: JOHN (X) GRISHAM. Wit: A. HUGHES, JAMES DICKINSON, ROBERT BAKER. . .BARBURY GRISHAM, wife of JOHN GRISHAM releases her right of dower.

Pages 298, 299. 18 February 1782. WILLIAM MEAD, attorney for NICHOLAS HAILE, sells to ISHAM BLANKENSHIP for the sum of sixty pounds the remainder of said HAILE'S land as Favl (?) ground branch after 52 acres laid off for STEPHEN HEARD and 165 acres to JOHN HORD about 580 acres more or less beginning at JOHN HORD'S corner in the patent line. Signed: W. MEAD. Wit: JAMES (X) DILLEN, ISHAM (X) BLANKENSHIP, ELIJAH (X) BLANKENSHIP.

Pages 299, 300. 19 March 1783. Deed of Gift. DANIEL NEWMAN of the county of Henry to JOHN NEWMAN, his brother of the same county, for the love and good will he beareth to his brother hath given, granted unto the said JOHN NEWMAN one parcel of land on the waters of Stone's Creek beginning one of the lines at KOGAR'S land containing 36½ acres. JOHN NEWMAN now lives on this land. Signed: DANIEL NEWMAN.

Wit: JOHN WATSON, ROBERT ELLISON, BOWLES ABBINGTON.

Pages 300, 301. 27 March 1783. Power of Attorney. FRANCIS SMITH of the county of Bedford do hereby appoint, constitute and ordain my trusty friend WILLIAM YOUNG of Essex County my true and lawful attorney to ask, demand and receive for me in my name and to have sole power to act for me. To sell a parcel of land belonging to me lying near said WILLIAM YOUNG'S in Essex County. Signed: FRANCIS SMITH.

Pages 301, 302. 27 March 1783. EUSEBUS HUBBARD of the county of Henry to THOMAS BOULTON of same for the sum of ten pounds sells land on the south side of Snow Creek ____ acres. Signed: EUSEBUS HUBBARD.

Pages 302, 303. 15 February 1783. ALEXANDER JOYCE of the county of Henry to GEORGE HAIRSTON for the sum of one hundred pounds sells and conveys land in the amount of 250 acres on the branches of Marrowbone Creek beginning at HENRY MAYS' dividing line, joins MCKAIN'S. Signed: ALEXANDER JOYCE. Wit: D. LANIER, DANIEL GOOLSBY, CHURCHILL BLAKEY, JOHN EAST.

Page 304. Inquisition. Inquisition for the Commonwealth of Virginia indented and taken 18 January 1783 before JOHN FONTAINE, JOHN SANFORD, GEORGE SANFORD, WILLIAM MORE, WILLIAM SWANSON, JR., JARED BURCH, JOHN ALEXANDER, GEORGE REYNOLDS, ROBERT PEDIGRUE, REUBEN NANCE, JOHN ACUFF, JOHN CONAWAY, JOHN MINTER, WILLIAM TACKITT, JOSEPH GRAVELY, THOMAS WILLSON, PHILIP BUSHEARS, JAMES MELTON, DANIEL WILSON, FRANCIS COX, SAMPSON MAXEY and THOMAS EDWARDS. WILLIAM RICE of the county of Henry was lawfully seized in his messuage on Smith River which land said RICE leased in 1775-76 for ten years in succession to HUMPHREY SCOGGINS and in 1781 said SCOGGINS leased the remainder of the ten years lease to MAJOR JOHN HAMPTON of whom said WILLIAM RICE as the jury determined by lawful contract purchased three years being the remainder of the said lease which expired 1 January last and therefore possession of land should be the priviledge of the said WILLIAM RICE, but a certain NIMROD MORRIS with strong hands hold possession from the first of January and continues to hold same and doth keep out said WILLIAM RICE to a great disturbance of the peace of the Commonwealth.

Pages 305, 306. 8 March 1783. JAMES EAST, SENR. and his wife ELLPHAN of the county of Henry to BENJAMIN KENNON for the sum of five pounds sell and convey land on Horsepasture Creek adjoining a tract surveyed by COX on part of which said KENNON now resides, near KOGERS Road containing 106 acres. Signed: JAMES EAST. Wit: JOHN WATSON, JOHN SALMON, BOWLES ABBINGTON.

Page 307. 27 March 1783. JOHN COOPER of the county of Henry to THOMAS MATHEWS for and in consideration of two likely negroes JOHN COOPER grants, sells and conveys unto said THOMAS MATHEWS land on the waters of Beaver Creek being 420 acres more or less joining the lines of JOSEPH ANTHONY and Little Beaver Creek. Signed: JOHN COOPER.

Page 308. Release of right of dower. RICHARD DICKINS sold 594 acres to BENJAMIN NEAL and as MARY DICKINS, wife of said RICHARD cannot conveniently travel to the Courthouse hereby relinquishes her right of dower.

Page 309. 15 February 1783. JAMES INGRUM of the county of Henry to WILLIAM WALDEN, JR. sells and conveys for the sum of thirty pounds 50 acres of land joining lines of WILLIAM MARTIN, HENRY SUMPTER and HALEY. Signed: JAMES (X) INGRUM, MARTHEW (MARTHA) (X) INGRUM. Wit: PETER BAYS, NATHAN (X) WALDEN, JOSEPH WALDEN.

Page 310. 17 September 1782. ROWLAND H. BIRK of the county of Henry formerly of Pittsalwany to JOSEPH WALDEN, SR. for and in consideration of a bond of PETER BAYS sells and conveys 99 acres of land on _____ Creek. Signed: ROWLAND HORSLEY BIRK. Wit: NOLAN (X) WALDEN, JAMES (X) INGRUM, WILLIAM (X) MARTIN, SARAH (X) WALDEN. . .SARAH, wife of R. H. BIRK relinquishes her right of dower.

Pages 311, 312. 24 March 1783. JOSEPH WEBSTER of the county of Henry to WILLIAM MEDLOCK of same for fifty pounds sells land on north side of Smith River. Signed: JOSEPH WEBSTER.

Pages 312, 313. 5 August 1782. DANIEL MCBRIDE of the county of Henry to JOHN HALEY for the sum of twenty pounds sells land containing 100 acres more or less on the branches of Leatherwood Creek, joins WILLIAMS path and MCBRIDE'S path. Signed: DANIEL (X) MCBRIDE. Wit: SILAS WILLIAMS, JOHN

BRISTOW, SAMUEL WATSON.

Pages 314, 315. 27 November 1782. JIMMY and JOHN JAMES of the county of Henry to RICHARD RENNOLDS for the sum of sixty pounds sell and convey 400 acres on Shooting Creek, beginning at the fork of Turkey Cock Creek on both sides, crosses Rackoon Branch. Signed: JIMMY JAMES, JOHN JAMES.

Pages 315, 316. 24 April 1783. JOHN EAST, heir at law of WILLIAM EAST, deceased of the county of Henry to JAMES REA for the sum of forty five pounds sells land on Little Marrowbone Creek containing by estimate 100 acres more or less, joins POOL'S branch commonly called Blevins, GRAY'S order line. This land which was conveyed by NATHAN HALL unto said WILLIAM EAST (in his lifetime) by deed recorded in Henry County. Signed: JOHN EAST. Wit: JOHN GRIGGORY, JOHN COX, GEORGE WALLER, JOHN SALMON, JOHN FONTAINE, MICHL. ROWLAND.

Pages 317, 318. 8 September 1781. SAMUEL FOX and MARY his wife to JOHN HUFF of the county of Henry for the sum of forty five pounds sell and convey land being 119 acres by patent dated at Richmond 1 September 1780, on Little Otter Creek with lines of CHRISTOPHER CHOATS. Signed: SAMEUL (X) FOX, MARY FOX. Wit: WILLIAM MAVITY, ELIJAH JONES, JACOB TROUPE, MARY MAVITY.

Pages 319, 320. 25 April 1783. ADAM LACKEY of the county of Henry to OBEDIAH DICKINSON for the sum of twenty five pounds land on Rock Castle Creek being 70 acres joins WALTON'S line.

Pages 320, 321. 7 December 1782. JOHN SIMMONS of the county of Henry to THOMAS BOULDIN of the county of Charlotte for the sum of one hundred fifty pounds land on both sides Grassy Creek of Smith River containing 585 acres. Signed: JOHN (X) SIMMONS, ANN (X) SIMMONS. Wit: JOHN PACE, JAMES REA, JOHN ALEXANDER.

Pages 322, 323. 24 April 1783. DARBY RYAN of Henry County to JOEL HARBOUR of the same for the sum of twenty five pounds sells part of a tract of land on both sides of Widgen Creek containing 135 acres more or less beginning at Harbour's corner poplar. Signed: DARBY RYAN. Wit: JAMES LYON, BRICE MARTIN, MORDECAI HORD.

Pages 324, 325. 24 April 1783. DARBY RYAN of Henry County to ESAIAS HARBOUR of the same for the sum of twenty five pounds sells part of a tract of land on the waters of Irvin (Smith) River being 135 acres more or less. Signed: DARBY RYAN. Wit: JAMES LYON, BRICE MARTIN, MORDECAI HORD.

Pages 325, 326. 24 April 1783. THOMAS PRUNTY and MARY his wife of Henry County to ABRAHAM VANDEVENTER for sum of one hundred fifty pounds sell land containing 249 acres on waters of Snow Creek, whereon THOMAS PRUNTY formerly live. Beginning at line that divides JOSEPH LEWIS' 105 acres from this part of the tract now sold, crosses south fork of Gutterys Run and CHOICE'S line. Signed: THOMAS PRUNTY. Wit: HUGH INNES, WILLIAM CHOICE, W. RYAN.

Pages 327, 328. October 1782. RICHARD DICKINS of the county of Henry to BENJAMIN NEAL of the same for the sum of one hundred pounds sells and conveys land in the amount of 388 acres more or less beginning at a dividing line, being part of a division sold to DANIEL RICE. Signed: RICHARD DEAKINS. Wit: JOHN MARR, WILLIAM SMITH, JAMES PIGG.

Pages 329, 330. 27 October 1782. RICHARD DICKINS of Henry County to DANIEL RICE of the same for the sum of forty five pounds sells 206 acres with lines of GRAY, being part of a dividend sold BENJAMIN NEAL. Signed: RICHARD DEAKINS. Wit: (same as above deed).

Pages 331, 332. 24 March 1783. ALEXANDER MCKEEN of Guilford County, North Carolina to JOHN KING of Henry County, Virginia for the sum of fifty pounds sells and conveys 147 acres on the east side of Marrowbone Creek with the lines of ROBERT CHANDLER. Signed: ALEXAND MCKEEN. Wit: DAVID LANIER, MILES HICKS, JAMES JOHNSON.

Pages 333, 334. 22 May 1783. MICHAEL ROWLAND of Henry County to JOHN BARKSDALE of the same for the sum of one hundred pounds sells all that parcel or tract of land on the waters of Town Creek and Chestnut Creek being 554 acres more or less conveyed to ROWLAND by JURIAH HOLCOMB administratrix of GRYMES HOLCOMB deceased, by deed recorded Henry County. Signed: MICHAEL ROWLAND.

Pages 334, 335. 17 April 1783. JAMES COOLEY of

Henry County to ABEL EDWARDS of the same for the sum of one hundred fifty pounds sells and conveys 183 acres more or less on both sides of a north branch of Snow Creek. Signed: JAMES COOLY (X), ANN (X) COOLY, his wife. Wit: PETER HODGES, HOLDEN MCGHEE, SAMUEL PATTERSON, WILLIAM (X) DELANHAM.

Pages 336, 337. 10 October 1782. THOMAS NUNN of Henry County to HENRY BARKSDALE and JOHN BARKSDALE for the sum of sixty five pounds doth sell unto HENRY BARKSDALE during his natural life and after his death unto said JOHN BARKSDALE a tract, piece or parcel of land on Irvin (now called Smith) River being 19 acres more or less, this land conveyed to said THOMAS NUNN by THOMAS M. RANDOLPH by deed recorded Henry County. Signed: THOMAS NUNN. Wit: BRICE MARTIN, MICHAEL ROWLAND, UNITY MARTIN.

Page 338. I, STEPHEN HEARD, in consideration of forty pounds to him in hand paid hath in plain and open markett sold all his right, claim or title of all sums due him by the district of which he is a member. Viz: Sums by said district due by subscription or other ways for the publick hire of BRIENT TRENT a soldier for service unto DANIEL PERREMAN of the county of Henry, whom I also appoint my lawful attorney to act for me. Signed: STEPHEN HEARD. Wit: JAMES MASON, BARNES HOLLOWAY.

Pages 339, 340. 24 April 1783. JOSEPH HALE of the county of Henry to JACOB OLDAKERS of the same for fifty pounds sells land on both sides of the North Fork of Pigg River being 164 acres. Signed: JOSEPH HALE. Wit: THOMAS PRUNTY, THOMAS HALE, JAMES JONES.

Pages 340, 341. 24 June 1783. MICHAEL KELLY of the county of Henry to JACOB CLOWER of said county for the sum of ninety pounds sells, grants and conveys 465 acres of land on the branches of Nicholas Creek and Daniels Run. Signed: MICHAEL (X) KELLY. . .MARY KELLY, wife of MICHAEL relinquishes her right of dower. Wit: WILLIAM MAVITY, ROBERT MAVITY, MARY MAVITY.

Pages 342, 343. 21 April 1783. FRANCIS EASSON of Botetourte County to ISAAC BATES of Henry County for the sum of one hundred twenty pounds sells and conveys 135 acres on Blackwater River. Signed: FRANCIS EASON. Wit: JOSEPH SHOWERS PRICE, JOHN RENTFRO, STEPHEN LEE.

Pages 344, 345. 7 March 1783. JOHN GRISHAM, JR. of Henry County to SAMUEL CLARK of said county for the sum of two hundred pounds sells land in the amount of 350 acres on Spoon Creek joining PARR'S line. Signed: JOHN GRISHAM. Wit: A. HUGHES, JAMES DICKENSON, ROBERT BAKER.

Page 346. 24 July 1783. WALTER KING COLE of the county of Henry to PETER FRANCISCO of the county of Cumberland sells, grants and conveys for the sum of two hundred pounds one full undivided fourth part of a certain tract of land in Henry County on Grassy Creek called Poysoned Fields formerly the property of RANDOLPH, HARMER & KING, containing 890 acres more or less. Signed: WA. KING COLE.

Pages 347, 348. 18 February 1783. ROBERT WALTON, SENR. of the county of Charlotte to FREDERICK FULKERSON of the county of Henry sells and conveys for the sum of sixteen pounds two shillings land on the South Mayo River containing 161 acres being all the land the said WALTON has lying on the north side of the South Mayo River beginning at a black walnut near the mouth of Bear Branch. Signed: ROBERT WALTON. Wit: SAMUEL CLARKE, CHARLES BEAZLEY, THOMAS VERNON.

Pages 349, 350. 21 January 1783. STEPHEN HEARD of the county of Henry to WILLIAM TRENT of said county for the sum of ninety pounds sells 900 acres more or less of land beginning at HEARD'S line, ISAM BELCHER'S, WHITTNER'S order line, JAMASON'S corner, Timbird Ridge and crosses Cedar Run. Signed: STEPHEN HEARD. Wit: JOHN SHORT (?), JOHN HEARD, ELIZABETH HEARD.

Pages 350, 351. 24 June 1783. JESSE CLAY to ELISHA LYONS of Henry County grants, sells, conveys 232 acres of land for the sum of two hundred pounds on both sides of the Blackwater River, joins lines of: SAMUEL UNDERWOOD and COCKRAM. Signed: JESSE CLAY, MIRIAM (X) CLAY. Wit: WILLIAM COCKRAN, JAMES EDMUNDSON, DAVID BRASIER.

Pages 352, 353. 22 August 1783. THOMAS HUFF to ADAM LACKEY both of Henry County for the sum of one hundred ten pounds sells land being 165 acres more or less beginning at a great rock on the south side of Flat Creek running to CHART ISAM'S line. Signed: THOMAS HOFF, ELIZABETH HOFF. Wit: RICHARD PILSON, JOHN LEACHER.

Pages 353, 354. 24 April 1783. JOHN SHORT of the county of Henry, planter, to SAMUEL UNDERWOOD, planter, of the same county for the sum of forty five pounds sells land joining HOLLAWAY and HEARD on Blackwater River beginning with WILLIAM MIEDES old line joins Poplar Camp Creek. Signed: JOHN SHORT. Wit: JESSE CLAY, JESSE HEARD, JAMES MASON, STEPHEN HEARD.

Pages 355, 356. 24 April 1783. JOSEPH DAVIS of the county of Henry to BAILEY CARTER for the sum of ten pounds conveys land on the branches of Nicholas' Creek containing 189 acres more or less the land held by grant dated at Richmond 1 June 1782. Signed: JOSEPH DAVIS.

Pages 356, 357. 2 April 1783. JOHN MINTER and his wife SUSANNAH of the county of Henry to PATRICK HENRY of the said county for the sum of three hundred pounds sells, grants and conveys land on Leatherwood Creek, the western fork, containing 240 acres adjoining lands of Lomax & Company, JOHN ACUFF, REUBEN NANCE and JOHN CONWAY according to the ancient and long established lines and bounds. Signed: JOHN MINTER, SUSANAH MINTER. Wit: WILLIAM PARKS, JOSEPH PARKS, BAINABA YEALY.

Page 358. Bill of Sale. DANIEL PERRYMAN of the county of Henry and parish of Patrick have sold to MARKAM LOVELL of the same, all my right and title to a negroe woman named Rachel and her increase comprised in a Deed of Gift unto ROBERT LOVELL and SARAH his wife, WILLIAM LOVELL, SARAH LOVELL, MARY ANN LOVELL, MARKAM LOVELL, ANN MARTIN LOVELL, SAMUEL MOON LOVELL and DANIEL LOVELL bearing date 1 March 1769 and received in the county of King George 6 April 1769. For the consideration of forty five pounds I sell all my right and claim. Signed: DANIEL PERRYMAN. Wit: JOHN SALMON, WILLIAM LOVELL, JOHN (X) DILLINGHAM.

Pages 359, 360. 23 May 1783. Deed of Trust. JOHN WELLS to JAMES BAKER both of the county of Henry in consideration of twenty pounds on loan for the term of 20 days from this date conveyed and made a certain negroe boy about 14 years named Will is to work for the use of the said twenty pounds until 20 days is expired. Should JOHN WELLS fail to replace to JAMES BAKER the twenty pounds, then JAMES BAKER may sell at publick auction said boy, but any money over twenty pounds is to be paid to said WELLS.

Signed: JOHN WELLS. Wit: GEORGE HAIRSTON, JOHN SALMON, GEORGE ROWLAND, JR. . .Received 26 February 1783.

Pages 360, 361. 28 June 1783. JOHN KINSEY of Botetourte County to THOMAS PRUNTY of the county of Henry for the sum of forty pounds sells land which said KINSEY held by deed from WILLIAM MAVITY. Land is situated on the north branches of Pigg River and bounded by JONES' old line, DARBY RYAN to the top of Whistling Hill containing 366 acres by grant dated at Williamsburg 20 October 1769. Signed: JOHN KINSEY. Wit: WILLIAM COOK, THOMAS JONES, JR., WILLIAM DUNN.

Pages 362, 363. 28 August 1783. MARVEL NASH of the county of Henry to WILLIAM SHARP of said county for the sum of one hundred forty five pounds land on Prathor's fork of the Mayo River containing 216 acres beginning at a corner tree on JOHN PULLIAM'S path, to THOMAS LOCKART'S path. Signed: MARVEL NASH.

Pages 363, 364. 4 August 1783. Power of Attorney. I, JESSE WITT of the county of Henry being heir at law and assignee by a Deed of Gift recorded in Chesterfield County from SYLVANAS WEBB, deceased to me. The said SYLVANAS WEBB purchased a tract of land of GEORGE LUMPKIN formerly of Pittsylvania County for which he paid him fifty pounds cash and took his bond for making a good title to said land and GEORGE LUMPKIN failed to do so to my great injury. I certify that I have delivered unto HOLCOMB (HOLMAN) FREEMAN of the state of Georgia the said LUMPKIN'S bond and give him power of attorney to act for me as he shall think lawful for my redress. Signed: JESSE WITT. Wit: SAMUEL COLEMAN MORRIS, JOSEPH MORRIS, GREGORY DURHAM.

Pages 364, 365. 28 August 1783. MARVEL NASH of the county of Henry to RICHARD COLLIER of said county for the sum of one hundred fifty pounds sell land on Prator's fork of Mayo River containing by estimate 229 acres beginning at THOMAS LOCKHART'S path, joins JOHN PULLIAM'S path then according to courses and tenor of pattent. Signed: MARVEL NASH.

Pages 366, 367. 23 January 1783. JAMES TAYLOR of the county of Henry to JOHN MAY for the sum of one hundred fifty pounds sells and conveys land by estimate containing 119 acres, it being part of the JAMES TAYLOR tract on Marrowbone Creek adjoining the lines of SAMUEL LANIER and GEORGE ROWLAND. Signed: JAMES TAYLOR.

Pages 368, 369. 28 August 1783. BAILEY CARTER to JOSEPH CARTER both of the county of Henry for the sum of fifteen pounds sells, grants and conveys land on the waters of Little Outer Creek being 100 acres more or less. Signed: BAILEY CARTER.

Pages 370, 371. 26 July 1783. JOHN MARR of Henry County & THOMAS BEDFORD of the county of Charlotte of the one part to GEORGE HAIRSTON of the 2nd part for the sum of fifty pounds MARR and BEDFORD sell land on the south side of Smith River it being 126 acres. Signed: JOHN MARR, THOMAS BEDFORD, JR.

Pages 371, 372. 25 September 1783. DAVID HALEY of the county of Henry to HARRISON HOBART of said county for the sum of one hundred pounds sells land on the north side of Smith River opposite the mouth of Bowings Creek, it being 600 acres more or less. Signed: DAVID HALEY. . .ESTER HALEY, wife of DAVID HALEY relinquishes her right of dower.

Page 373. 17 September 1783. JOHN HEARD to WILLIAM BOYD both of Henry County, for the sum of forty five pounds HEARD sells land on Foul Ground Creek on the south side of Blackwater River joining GILLIAM'S line in the amount of 125 acres. Signed: JOHN HEARD. Wit: PETER GILLUM, STEPHEN HEARD, JESSE HEARD.

Page 374. 30 March 1783. Deed of Trust. DAVID HALEY of the one part to WILLIAM WILMOTH and HENRY SUMPTER of the other part. For divers good causes and considerations does convey and make over a tract, parcel or piece of land on Arvine (Irvine?) River, the land whereon I now live, also all other land in Henry County which I am legally possessed of to said WILMOTH and SUMPTER. Nevertheless, should DAVID HALEY comply with bond, then null and void. Signed: DAVID HALEY. Wit: JOHN SALMON, JOHN BARKSDALE, THADEUS SALMON.

Page 375. 24 July 1783. In obediance to an Order of the Court to survey and lay off prison bounds surveyed __ ½ acres the same is bounded by a white oak crossing the Spring Branch to a beech, etc. Signed: WILLIAM WOODS, according to JOHN DICKENSON.

Page 376. 29 March 1783. BAILEY CARTER of Henry

County to JOHN OAKES for the sum of eighteen pounds sells land on the waters of Nicholas Creek containing 100 acres joing PETER SAUNDERS. Signed: BAILEY CARTER. Wit: NATHAN HALL, DARBY RYAN, JOSEPH CARTER, JOHN CARTER.

Pages 377, 378. 23 September 1783. JOHN SIMMONS and NANCY his wife of Henry County to JOHN RENNO for the sum of eighty pounds sell and convey land on Grassey Creek, a branch of Irvin River containing 237 acres more or less with lines of JESSE WILLINGHAM and STEPHEN RENNO. Signed: JOHN (X) SIMMONS. . .NANCY SIMMONS relinquishes right of dower.

Pages 378, 379. 15 February 1783. JAMES INGRUM of the county of Henry to WILLIAM MARTIN for the sum of fifty pounds do hereby sell and convey 75 acres more or less on Goblingtown Creek, with ROLAND HORSLEE BIRKS' line to ROWLAND CHILES to DAVID HALEY'S to a creek. Signed: JAMES (X) INGRUM, MARTHEY (X) INGRUM. Wit: PETER BAYS, NATHANIEL (X) WALDEN, JOSEPH WALDEN.

Pages 379, 380. 27 March 1783. JAMES DICKENSON of the county of Henry to THOMAS COX of the county of Mecklingburg sells land containing 180 acres on the Muster Branch of Leatherwood Creek for the sum of ten pounds, joins: STEPHEN, BARNARD, REYNOLDS and FRANCIS COX. Signed: JOHN DICKINSON.

Pages 381, 382. 8 September 1783. ISHAM TALBERT of the county of Campbell to WILLIAM GREER of Henry County for the sum of twenty pounds sells land on both sides Little Bull Run containing 192 acres. Signed: ISHAM TALBOTT. Wit: JOHN DAVIS, STEPHEN HEARD, JESSE HEARD.

Pages 382, 383, 384. 25 September 1783. FREDERICK RIVES to THOMAS POTTER for the sum of twenty pounds does hereby sell and convey land on the south side of Pigg River containing by estimate 250 acres more or less with Walthan Order of Council, crosses Mountain Creek to an oak on Pigg River at the old road. Signed: FREDERICK RIVES.

Pages 385, 386. 21 August 1783. WILLIAM POOR of the county of Henry to ANDREW WOOLVERTON for the sum of twenty pounds sells 391 acres of land on the waters of Spoon Creek beginning at JOHN GRISHAM'S line and JOHN PARR'S. Signed: WILLIAM POOR. Wit: A. HUGHES, ROBERT BAKER, HAMON CRITZ.

Pages 387, 388. 25 September 1783. ANTHONY TITTLE of the county of Henry, Planter, to his son PETER TITTLE for the sum of ten pounds sells and grants land on a branch of Gobling Town Creek. Signed: ANTHONY TITTLE. Wit: MARK FOSTER.

Pages 388, 389. 25 September 1783. JOSEPH ANTHONY of Henry County to JACOB FARIS for the sum of one hundred twenty five pounds in goald or silver sells land in the amount of 200 acres more or less. Lines: THOMAS MITHIS, ANTHON BITTINGS, ROBERT DONALD, HENRY CLARK and Great Beaver Creek. Signed: JAMES ANTHONY.

Pages 390, 391. 10 March 1780. JAMES COWDEN of the county of Henry to SAMUEL PATTERSON for thirty pounds sells 470 acres more or less on the south side of Pigg River on side of Camp Creek. Signed: JAMES COWDAN. Wit: JONATHAN BAIRD, DANIEL EGGERS, JESSE CLAY, WILLIAM COWDAN, EONA CHILDRESS.

Pages 392, 393. 27 February 1783. Deed of Gift. JOSEPH KEELING of the county of Henry to JOHN ALEXANDER KEELING his son and FANNY ALEXANDER FRANKLIN(G) his daughter-in-law of the other part for the tender love and affection he hath for his son and daughter-in-law hath granted to them one negro woman slave called Hannah with her increase at the death of my wife ALICE at which time the said negroe and her increase be divided between them. I reserve the use of the said negroe during the life-time of my wife ALICE. The said negro not being present at the time of ensealing, the said JOSEPH KEELING delivered two pieces of silver in name of said negro to his son and daughter-in-law. Wit: GEORGE MARTIN, ELIZABETH (X) SAMMONS.

Pages 393, 394, 395. 16 September 1783. JAMES HEARD of the county of Henry to THOMAS HAMMON for the sum of fifty pounds conveys land on Jacks Creek containing in two pattents one for 290 acres bearing date 20 October 1779 and the other for 100 acres dated 10 April 1780 joining the former tract...being a total of 390 acres. Signed: THOMAS HEARD.

Pages 395, 396. 22 April 1782. EDWARD CHOAT of Henry County to WILLIAM BARTEE for the sum of ten pounds sells land on Doe Creek containing 485 acres by patent bearing date of 20 July 1780, it being above a branch called Bartee's Branch whereon said BARTEE now lives. Signed: EDWARD CHOAT.

Pages 397, 398. 23 April 1783. GEORGE CARTER of the county of Henry to HENRY ARNOLD for the sum of five pounds sells land being 127 acres by survey bearing date 18 October 1769 in County of Henry (formerly Pittsylvania) on the Bull Mountain (creek ?) a fork of the Mayo River. Signed: GEORGE CARTER. Wit: WILLIAM CARTER, DANIEL LAIN (?), MORMAN LAWSON.

Pages 398, 399. Bond. Bond of ROBERT HAIRSTON as Sheriff to collect taxes.

Page 400. 9 April 1783. JOHN BARKER of the county of Henry to JOHN HOLLAND of the county of Charlotte for the sum of seventy five pounds sells land at the mouth of a branch on the north side of Smith River containing 200 acres. Signed: JOHN (X) BARKER. Wit: ALEXANDER HUNTER, ESIAS HARBOUR, JOEL HARBOUR.

Pages 401, 402. 8 November 1783. JOSIAH CARTER of Henry County to GEORGE WALLER of said county for the sum of two hundred fifty pounds sells all that dividend tract on both sides of Reedy Creek and on the north side of Smith River containing 116 acres more or less and being part of a greater tract of 212 acres conveyed JOSIAH CARTER by THOMAS M. RANDOLPH by deed. Joins ROBERT DONALD and BAYNES CARTER. Signed: JOSIAH CARTER. Wit: JOHN PYRTLE, MICHAEL ROWLAND, JAMES JONES, JOHN NORRIS. . .MARY, wife of JOSIAH CARTER releases dower right. Recorded as paid two hundred eighty pounds.

Pages 403, 404. Power of Attorney. JOHN HAYNES of Bedford County for good causes we here unto moving made ordained and appoint BERNARD PRIMAN of Henry County attorney to demand, sue and recover from JOHN RED of Henry County a negro girl aged between 14-26 years or else sixty pounds specia also 300 acres of land all of which said JOHN RED doth stand justly indebted to me said JOHN HAYNES. Signed: JOHN (X) HAYNES. Wit: DANIEL PERRYMAN, JEHU PERRYMAN.

Pages 405-407. 21 October 1783. WILLIAM TUNSTALL of the county of Henry of the one part and A. HUGHES, HENRY LYNE and JOHN SALMON of the other part. Whereas the said TUNSTALL in a bond recorded in Henry County as executor of the estate of JOHN BLOGGE deceased and whereas the parties of the second part have become uneasy, fearing in a future day their heirs might become liable for their being bondsmen. Therefore, WILLIAM TUNSTALL puts up the following and shall remain as his security to wit: the following negroes: PETER, ROBIN, SARAH and 5 children, RACHEL, DOLL, JENNY, ROSE, MILLEY and 3 children, JOE, AMSY, JOHN, AGNESS and 6 children, SAM, LEWY, GEORGE, NELL, JACK and JAMMY son of Biddy. One dark bay horse. Until such a time as the end of his executorship and the end of their security for his bond. Signed: WILL. TUNSTALL. Wit: JOHN COX, WALTER LAMB.

Pages 407, 408. 21 October 1783. FILNOR GREEN of Henry County to JOHN KEEN for a sartain sum sells a sartain tract of land containing 800 acres more or less on the north side of Pigg River, joins WILLIAM HALL. Signed: PHILMOR GREEN. Wit: WILLIAM RYAN, ROBERT MASON, JOHN BARSDILL, JOHN COX.

Pages 409, 410. January 1784. Bond of ABRAHAM PENN constituted and appointed Sheriff to collect tax and account for such. Signed: A. PENN, JAMES SHELTON, bondsmen, JOSEPH ANTHONY, ROBERT STOCKTON, JOHN BARKSDALE, ALEXANDER HUNTER. Wit: JAMES ANTHONY, ANTHONY BITTING, JOHN STOKES, PETER LEAK, GEORGE HAMILTON, JOHN REDD.

Page 411. Is a duplicate of pages 409, 410.

Pages 412, 413. 21 March 1783. DANIEL FORD and MOLLY his wife to JESSE DILLINGHAM for the sum of twenty three pounds ten shillings sells and conveys land on Marrowbone Creek, a branch of Irvin River containing 50 acres more or less bounded by JOHN RICHARDSON, JESSE DILLINGHAM, JOHN HARDMAN. Signed: DANIEL FORD, MOLLY FORD. Wit: JOHN RENNO, JAMES SCRUGS, JOHN HARDMAN, WILLIAM FEWEL.

Page 414. WILLIAM WHITSITT of the county of Henry for and in consideration of the love and goodwill I have for my daughter and son-in-law WILLIAM BRETHEAD of Henry County give and bequeath them part of 2 tracts on Little Beaver Creek I bought of COL. ABRAM PENN, adjoining ROBERT STOCKTON containing 300 acres more or less. Signed: WILLIAM WHITSITT. Wit: ROBERT STOCKTON, WILLIAM FRENCH, JOHN WATSON.

Page 415, 416. 28 January 1784. WILLIAM LOVELL of Henry County to WILLIAM BREATHEART of the same county for the sum of one hundred pounds sells land on both sides of Beaver Creek adjoining the lands of THOMAS and JOSEPH COOPER, by estimate 100 acres more or less which was conveyed LOVELL by MARVEL NASH, deed recorded in Henry County. Signed: WILLIAM LOVELL. Wit: JOHN COX, GEORGE HAIRSTON, JOHN NEWMAN.

Pages 416-418. 29 October 1783. Deed of Trust. WILLIAM TUNSTALL to JOHN FONTAINE and GEORGE HAIRSTON, whereas WILLIAM TUNSTALL had as bondsmen the above when he was appointed executor of the estate of JOHN ROWLAND, deceased; now they are uneasy as TUNSTALL has not fully accounted for the estate and fearing for their secutity-ship and WILLIAM TUNSTALL desiring to make them safe, puts up as security the following slaves: BIDDY, NED, SANDY, PATT, SARAH, JOHN, DOLLY, LEWIS, ROBIN, RACHEL, and POLLY. Signed: WILL. TUNSTALL. Wit: P. HENRY, WAT. LAMB, JOHN PYRTLE.

Pages 419, 420. 13 January 1784. GEORGE ROWLAND and ANN his wife to GEORGE HAIRSTON for the sum of one hundred ninety five pounds sells and conveys 300 acres of land more or less on the north side of Marrowbone Creek beginning at the mouth of Sinking Branch joining lines of JAMES TAYLOR, SAMUEL LANIER and SHAW. Signed: GEORGE ROWLAND, ANN (X) ROWLAND. Wit: JOSIAS SHAW, BENJAMIN HELMS, BENJAMIN THOMAS.

Pages 421, 422, 423. 26 February 1784. PHILLIP THOMAS and MARY his wife to GEORGE HAIRSTON for the sum of one hundred thirty pounds sells land containing by patent 337 acres more or less on the Smith River on the south side beginning at RANDOLPH & Company line, JOHN BLEVINS corner, to first station; was patented to WILLIAM BLEVINS, SR., being 125 acres, survey made by PHILLIP THOMAS. Signed: PHILLIP THOMAS.

Pages 423, 424, 425. JESSE WILLINGHAM (DILLINGHAM) and FANY his wife to GEORGE HAIRSTON for the sum of one hundred fifty pounds land on the head branches of Marrowbone Creek, a branch of Smith River being 300 acres more or less with lines of JOHN HARDMAN, JOHN RENNO, URIAH HARDMAN, JOHN RICHARDSON and touching land formerly owned by ELLINER TORBORNE and DANIEL FORD. Signed: JESSE WILLING-

HAM, FANNY (X) WILLINGHAM. When deed recorded listed as DILLINGHAM.

Pages 425, 426. 23 March 1784. STEPHEN HEARD to MARTIN BENNION for the sum of twenty pounds conveys land containing 240 acres more or less on the branches of Blackwater River with lines of JESSE LAW, RICHARD PRIMONS, WHITIN. Signed: STEPHEN HEARD.

Pages 427, 428. 23 March 1784. STEPHEN HEARD to MARTIN BINNION for the sum of fifty pounds sells land containing 342 acres by survey, on Blackwater River with lines of DILLON and JOHN HEARD. Signed: STEPHEN HEARD.

Pages 428, 429. 23 September 1783. ROBERT HAMPTON and MARY his wife to ISAAC MCDONALD for the sum of one hundred ninety pounds sells one parcel of land being part of the JAMES TAYLOR survey. In Henry County on both sides of No Business fork of the Mayo River containing by estimate 200 acres. Signed: ROBERT HAMPTON, MARY (X) HAMPTON. Wit: JAMES TAYLOR, SAMUEL SMITH, JOHN HORRELL.

Pages 429, 430. Dower release. MARY, wife of PHILLIP THOMAS cannot conveniently travel to the Courthouse therefore the Justices accept her release of her right to dower in the sale of land to GEORGE HAIRSTON, as to be her true account without duress. 10 March 1784.

Page 431. 10 March 1784. Dower release. ANN ROWLAND, wife of GEORGE ROWLAND seperately and apart from her husband without threat or persecution does voluntarily release her right of dower.

Page 432. 11 March 1784. Dower release. FANNY WILLINGHAM, wife of JESSE release right of dower to land sold GEORGE HAIRSTON.

Pages 433, 434. 26 March 1784. WILLIAM BARTEE of Henry County to JAMES PARBERY for the sum of forty seven pounds ten shillings sells one moriety of a tract of land on Doe Creek containing 485 acres by patent bearing date 20 July 1780. With lines of CHOATS to BARTEE'S branch, whereon BARTEE now lives. Signed: WILLIAM BARTEE. . .MARY, the wife of WILLIAM BARTEE relinquishes her right of dower.

Pages 434, 435. 25 March 1784. HENRY JONES TO ISIAH

WILLIS for the sum of one hundred pounds sells land on Pigg River it being 498 acres more or less with lines of ROBERT JONES, How Branch and the line near Whistling Hill. Signed: HENRY JONES. Wit: ELIJAH JONES, ROBERT JONES, JESSE JONES. . .FRANKEY, the wife of HENRY JONES relinquishes her right of dower.

Pages 436, 437. 6 March 1784. HENRY JONES of Henry County to DAVID PEW for the sum of sixty pounds sells and conveys all messuages, tenaments and parcel of land containing 160 acres on both sides of the head branch of Pigg River under the foot of the Blue Ridge. Patent of which land bears date 10 September 1777. Signed: HENRY JONES.

Pages 437, 438. November 1783. JOEL BARKER of the county of Henry to ABRAHAM PENN for the sum of fifty pounds sells land on the branches of the Mayo River containing 288 acres, beginning at LYNCH'S corner, DICKENS and RANDOLPH'S lines. Signed: JOELL BARKER. Wit: ISAAC MCDONALD, CHARLES HIBBERT, WILLIAM (X) SHARP.

Pages 439, 440. 16 September 1783. HENRY JONES of Henry County to SAMUEL MILES for the sum of fifty pounds sells and conveys 340 acres of land, by grant bearing date at Williamsburg 20 October 1779, it being on the Draughts of Pigg River with lines of JOHN JONES and ABRAM JONES. Signed: HENRY JONES. . .FRANKEY, wife of HENRY JONES relinquishes her right of dower.

Pages 440, 441. 22 March 1784. JOHN SIMS of the county of Henry and state of North Carolina (?) to HENRY FRANCE of the county of Henry and state of Virginia, for the sum of fifty pounds sells land containing 100 acres more or less on Crooked Creek and on both sides of the South Mayo River, being part of a patent bearing date 1 March 1781, joins FONTAINES' corner. Signed: JOHN SIMS.

Page 442. 8 March 1784. JOHN HARDMAN and ELIZABETH his wife of Henry County to JOHN SIMMONS for the sum of one hundred fifty pounds sells land on Marrowbone Creek, a branch of Smith River, containing by estimate 150 acres with lines of SAMUEL LANIER, JOHN RICHARDSON, GEORGE HAIRSTON and land formerly belonging to JESSE WILLINGHAM. Signed: JOHN (X) HARDMAN. Wit: ISIAS SHAW, ALEXANDER JOYCE, JAMES EAST.

Page 443. 27 September 1781. STEPHEN HEARD of Henry

County to JOHN JAMISON for the sum of fifty pounds sells land on the branches of Simmons Creek being 71 acres more or less, crosses the ridge between Pigg River and Blackwater River joins WITTONS order line. Signed: STEPHEN HEARD. Wit: RICHARD PERRYMAN, JESSE HEARD.

Page 444. 11 September 1783. BENJAMIN HICK of the county of Greensville to ALEXANDER JOYCE of the county of Henry for the sum of three hundred pounds sells and conveys all messuages, orchards, and land on the north side of Marrowbone Creek (no acreage given). Signed: BENJAMIN HICKS. Wit: D. LANIER, JOHN KING, MILES HICKS.

Page 445. 25 March 1784. SAMUEL ALLEN of the county of Henry to WILLIAM MCPEAK for the sum of twenty five pounds sells land on both sides of the north fork of Jack's Creek containing by estimate 107 acres. Signed: SAMUEL ALLEN.

Page 446. 17 October 1783. AMOS RICHARDSON of the county of Henry to MARTHA BAILEY for the sum of twenty pounds sells land on Buck Branch of Snow Creek containing by estimate 100 acres beginning at JOHN RICHARDSON corner. Signed: AMOS RICHARDSON.

Pages 447, 448. 25 March 1784. JOHN BARKER of Henry County to JOHN DAY for the sum of one hundred pounds sells land being 258 acres more or less on the north fork of Spoon Creek with REYNOLDS line. Signed: JOHN (X) BARKER.

Page 449. 17 October 1783. AMOS RICHARDSON of Henry County to BENJAMIN COOK for the sum of seventy pounds sells land on the Grassy fork of Snow Creek containing 280 acres more or less joining WILLIAM RYAN. Signed: AMOS RICHARDSON.

Page 450. 22 March 1784. JOHN SIMS of the County of Surry and state of North Carolina to FREDERICK HUTCHENS of the county of Henry for the sum of twenty five pounds sells land containing 72 acres more or less on the south side of Mayo River, it being part of a land grant to SIMS by patent dated 1 March 1781, joins lines of HENRY FRANCE. Signed: JOHN SIMS.

Pages 451, 452. 26 November 1783. WILLIAM STEGGALL to AMOS RICHARDSON for the sum of fifty pounds sells land on the Mountain Fork of Snow Creek with lines of TULLY CHOICE and ABRAHAM ARDON, it being 200 acres more or less, being part of 800 acres granted by patent 27 August 1783. Signed: WILLIAM STEAGALL. Wit: JAMES PRUNTY, BOTOM ESTES, THOMAS TOWNSON.

Page 452. 10 June 1782. Pittsylvania County. I do hereby relinquish right, title, etc unto 200 acres of land in Henry County which I bought at publick sale being formerly the property of WILLIAM STEGALL and sold by deed of trust made unto WALTER ROBERTSON. Signed: SAMUEL CALLAND.

Page 453. 25 March 1784. JOHN BARKER, SR. and his wife of Henry County to JESSE REYNOLDS for the sum of one hundred pounds sell land on the north fork of Spoon Creek containing by estimate 200 acres. Joins line of WARD. Signed: JOHN (X) BARKER.

Page 454. 24 March 1784. AMOS RICHARDSON of Henry County to WILLIAM VINCENT for the sum of thirty five pounds sells 100 acres land on the south side of Snow River. Signed: AMOS RICHARDSON. . .MARTHA, wife of AMOS RICHARDSON relinquishes right of dower.

Page 455. 16 September 1783. JOHN SHORT of the county of Henry to JOHN MARCUM, late of Bedford County, Virginia for the sum of fifty pounds sells 170 acres on Blackwater River, crosses Poplar Camp Creek and joins WILLIAM HEARD. Signed: JOHN SHORT, STEPHEN HEARD. Wit: THOMAS MARCUM, WILLIAM (X) MARCUM, JOHN (X) TIRA (?).

Pages 456, 457. 21 October 1783. ARCHELAUS HUGHES and JOHN WIMBISH of the one part to ANTHONY SMITH of the county of Henry for the sum of twenty five pounds sell 100 acres on Soctons Branch of the Mayo River, with RANDOLPH'S line. Singed: A. HUGHES, JOHN WIMBISH. Wit: HAYNES MORGAN, JOHN SALMON, R. WILLIAMS.

Pages 457, 458. 21 October 1783. A. HUGHES and JOHN WIMBISH to JOHN PULLIAM and JOHN RANDAL for the sum of seventy five pounds sells land on the north fork of Mayo River containing 180 acres. Signed: A. HUGHES, JOHN WIMBISH.

Page 459. 5 March 1784. DEVERIX GILLIAM and EADIA, his wife in consideration of two negros sells 250 acres of land more or less on the south side, of Little Mayo River, beginning at the mouth of

THOMAS SMITH'S spring branch, HAMON CRITZ line.
Signed: DEVERIX GILLIAM.

Page 460. 22 April 1784. JAMES INGRUM of the county of Henry to JOSEPH STREET for the sum of fifty pounds sells 50 acres of land beginning at CLONCHES line to WILLIAM MARTIN'S line to WILLIAM WALDEN and ANTHONY INGRUM. Signed: JAMES INGRUM, MARTHA (PATTEY) INGRUM.

Page 461. 22 April 1784. JOHN RICHARDSON of the county of Henry to JOHN ABINGTON, SR. for the sum of twenty pounds sells land on the waters of Horsepasture Creek, lines: WALTON, LAYNE, RANDOLPH & Co. containing 259 acres. Signed: JOHN (X) RICHARDSON.

Pages 462, 463. 14 September 1773. JAMES RENTFRO of the county of Pittsylvania to JAMES CALLAWAY of the county of Bedford for the sum of five hundred twenty five pounds sells land containing 400 acres more or less and being in Pittsylvania County on both sides of Blackwater River. Signed: JAMES RENTFROE. Wit: GROSS SCRUGGS, ROBERT JONES, JAMES RENTFROE,JR. . .Acknowledged: CALEB TATE, BRUKES SMITH 10 Sept. 1775. . .Acknowledged: STEPHEN SMITH, JOSEPH TALER. . .ESTER RENTFRO, wife of JAMES RENTFRO relinquishes her right of dower.

Page 464. 16 September 1783. Power of Attorney. MILES JENNINGS of the county of Henry appoints my friend HENRY FRANCE my lawful attorney. Signed: MILES JENNINGS. Wit: A. HUGHES, JOHN SCHNEES (?), THOMAS JOHNSON.

Pages 464, 465. 7 April 1784. WILLIAM YOUNG of the county of Pittsylvania to LEWIS POTTER of Henry County for the sum of twenty pounds sells and conveys 40 acres more or less on the south side of Pigg River joins ROBERT BOULTON and ABNER COCKRAN. Signed: WILLIAM YOUNG. Wit: BENJAMIN POTTER, ROBERT BOULTON.

Pages 465, 466. 22 April 1784. GEORGE WALLER of the county of Henry to JOHN REDD of the same for the sum of two hundred eighty pounds sells and conveys all that tract on both sides of Reedy Creek and on the north side of Smith River containing 116 acres more or less being part of a granter tract of 212 acres conveyed unto JOSIAH CARTER by THOMAS M. RANDOLPH by deed recorded in Henry County, then CARTER to WALLER. The 116 acres bounded by ROBERT

DONALD and BAYNES CARTER. Signed: GEORGE WALLER.

Page 467. 22 April 1784. STEPHEN SENTER of the county of Pittsylvania to THOMAS TERRY of Henry County for divers good causes and eighty pounds sells and conveys land containing 216 acres in the County of Henry on the branches of Turkey Cock Creek joining lines of WILLIAM YOUNG. Signed: STEPHEN (X) SENTER, SUSANNAH SENTER. Wit: AARON MACKINZIE, ARCHBALD YOUNG, ALLEN RIDLEY YOUNG.

Page 468. 22 April 1784. SAMUEL WATSON and PHEEBE his wife of the county of Henry to JOSEPH PEREGOY for the sum of five pounds sells and conveys 50 acres more or less on the branches of Beaver Creek. Signed: SAMUEL (X) WATSON, PHEEBE (X) WATSON. Wit: JOHN MCCONNAWAY, JOHN MINTER, BETSAY CONNAWAY.

Page 469. 22 April 1784. JAMES INGRUM of Henry County to ROWLAND CHILES for the sum of twenty pounds conveys 40 acres of land joins: BARTLET FOLEY, HALEY, JEREMIAH CLAUNCHE. Signed: JAMES (X) INGRUM. . .MARTHA INGRUM, wife of JAMES relinquishes her right of dower.

Page 470. 7 December 1782. THOMAS BUSH of the county of Henry to PETER HAIRSTON of the same for the sum of three hundred pounds sells and conveys 100 acres more or less on the south side of Little Marrowbone Creek beginning at RANDOLPH, HARMER and KINGS order line. Includes plantation the said BUSH now lives on, it being part of a larger tract patent to RANDOLPH, HARMER & KING. Signed: THOMAS BUSH. Wit: GEORGE HAIRSTON, RUEBEN PAYNE, WILLIAM HORD.

Pages 471, 472. 22 August 1783. MARVEL NASH of the county of Henry to JOHN WATSON for the sum of eighty pounds sells land patented to ADAM LACKEY and deeded to MARVEL NASH containing 900 acres, which tract said MARVEL NASH oblidges himself to contain 800 acres. Reference to the above deed for further description. Signed: MARVEL NASH. Wit: WILLIAM WOODS, BOWLES ABINGTON, WILLIAM FRENCH. . .AGNESS NASH, wife of MARVEL NASH relinquishes her right of dower.

Pages 472, 473. 22 August 1783. MARVEL NASH of the county of Henry to JOHN WATSON for the sum of fifty pounds sells 302 acres on the north side of the North Mayo River and Cogers Creek lying betwix MIAH PRATOR and THOMAS LOCKHART. Signed:

* Deed pages 473-474 omitted. See page 111.

THOMAS MATHEWS.

Pages 474, 475. 7 April 1784. JAMES STANDIFORD of the county of Henry to MORDECAI MOSSELY for the sum of forty pounds sells and conveys 170 acres of land on Story Creek. Signed: JAMES (X) STANDEFER. Wit: JOHN FERGUSON, WILLIAM WEAKES, JAMES STANDEFER, JR.

Pages 475, 476. 13 September 1783. JESSE WITT of the county of Henry to HENRY MAYSE for the sum of fifty pounds sells land by estimate 150 acres, beginning at a black oak on the south side of Fall Creek at DAVID WITT'S corner. Signed: JESSE WITT. Wit: DRURY SMITH, WILLIAM HAYSE, JOHN (X) JONNIKIN.

Pages 476, 477. Deed of Gift. I, JAMES MENESE, of the county of Pittsylvania for the love and affection I bear for my daughter ELENER WHITSITT of the county of Henry, at my decease and my wife's, do give her one negroe woman named Beck also fifty pounds specie and my desk. Signed: JAMES MENNES. Wit: JOSEPH ANTHONY, JACOB FERRIS, WILLIAM WHITSITT.

Pages 477, 478. 24 May 1784. THOMAS PRUNTY of the county of Henry to ZACHERIAH DAVIS for the sum of thirty pounds sells and conveys land, being 165 acres on the branches of Pigg River, it being part of a tract patented in the name of WILLIAM MAVITY. Signed: THOMAS PRUNTY.

Page 479. 24 May 1784. WILLIAM FERGUSON of Henry County to DAVID JONES for the sum of five pounds ten shillings conveys land on Pigg River containing 81 acres. Signed: WILLIAM FERGUSON. Wit; THOMAS HILL, ELIJAH JONES, SABROT CHOAT.

Pages 480, 481. 23 November 1784. FRANCIS KERBY of the county of Fluvanna to BOTTOM ESTES of Henry County for the sum of one hundred pounds sells 275 acres of land being on the head of Bull Run, joins DAVIS' line. Signed: FRANCIS KEARBY. Wit: JESSE KEARBY, STEPHEN LOY, JAMES HUBBARD.

Page 482. 27 October 1783. THOMAS M. RANDOLPH, GEORGE HARMER and WALTER KING COLE to ABRAHAM PENN for the sum of one thousand pounds sells land on the south side of Smith River, containing by patent 290 acres, beginning at the mouth of Jordon's Creek. Signed: THOMAS M. RANDOLPH, GEORGER HARMER,

WM. KING COLE. Wit: HUGH INNES, GEORGE HAIRSTON, PETER SAUNDERS, WILLIAM MCCRUMP, THOMAS LIVESY, JOSHUA CANTRALL.

Pages 483, 484. 27 October 1783. THOMAS M. RANDOLPH, GEORGE HARMER, WALTER KING COLE to ABRAHAM PENN for the sum of two thousand pounds sells land on both sides of the North Mayo River containing by patent 1,155 acres. . .Same witness as above.

Page 485. 29 September 1783. JAMES EDWARDS of the county of Henry to ROWLAND SALMON for the sum of thirty pounds sells and conveys land on the waters of Smith River containing 142 acres, beginning at SELLIRES (SILAS) RATLIF'S corner, BENJAMIN HUBBARD'S line, JOHN SNEED'S line. Signed: JAMES (X) EDWARDS, ELIZABETH (X) EDWARDS. Wit: BENJAMIN HUBBARD, JESSE HUBBARD, JAMES (X) BRAMER, SILES (X) RATLIF.

Pages 486, 487. 25 May 1784. RICHARD REYNOLDS of the county of Henry to WILLIAM EDWARDS for the sum of one hundred pounds sells and conveys 400 acres of land on Shooting Creek, beginning at a walnut in the fork of Turkey Cock Creek, crosses Rackoon Branch. Signed: RICHARD (X) REYNOLDS.

Pages 487, 488. 7 November 1783. ROBERT BAKER of the county of Henry to WILLIAM GRAY for the sum of one hundred fifty pounds sells and conveys 479 acres of land, 119½ acres being part of ROBERT WALTON'S order of council, on both sides of Green Creek and on Mayo River and all that part of said order that lyes between THOMAS LOWS and NATHANIEL SCALES and MATHEW HOBSON. Signed: ROBERT BAKER. Wit: CHRISTOPHER STANLEY, AUGUSTIN THOMAS, A. HUGHES, WILLIAM MAYO.

Page 489. 4 March 1784. OBEDIAH DICKERSON of the county of Botetourt to GEORGE MABERY of the county of Henry for the sum of twenty pounds sells 70 acres of land on Rockcastle Creek beginning at WALTON'S south line. Signed: OBEDIAH (X) DICKERSON. Wit: JAMES CUTCHAM, DAVID KINZEY, JAMES KINZEY.

Page 490. 24 April 1784. JOSEPH ANTHONY of the county of Henry to HENRY CLARK for the sum of two hundred pounds sells 400 acres of land beginning at HOUSTON'S line, Beaver Creek with all appurtenances except 2 acres at the Mill. Signed: JOSEPH ANTHONY. Wit: JAMES ANTHONY, JACOB FERRIS, WILLIAM HUNTER.

Pages 491, 492. 23 June 1784. JOSEPH JONES of the county of Henry to WILLIAM STANDEFER for the sum of two hundred pounds sells all land, all messuages on both sides of Pigg River containing 50 acres in one tract and 54 acres in another tract joining the same with lines of BARTON and TURNER. Signed: JOSEPH JONES.

Page 492. 23 November 1784. FRANCIS KEARBY of the county of Fluvanna to STEPHEN LOY of Henry County for the sum of one hundred pounds sells and conveys a parcel of land containing 214 acres more or less lying on Olcat fork of Wins Creek. Signed: FRANCIS KEARBY. Wit: JESSE KEARBY, BOTTOM ESTES, JAMES HUBBARD.

Pages 493, 494. 24 June 1784. BAYNES CARTER and his wife MARTHA CARTER to GEORGE HAIRSTON for the sum of four hundred pounds sells and conveys land and all that is on it containing 221½ acres on Reed Creek being a branch of the Smith River. It being the tract conveyed from PETER COPLAND to MICHAEL ROWLAND which was bought of said COPLAND by BRADLEY MEREDITH. Signed: BAYNES CARTER.

Pages 495, 496. 22 July 1784. WILLIAM COOK of the county of Henry to PETER SANDERS of the same for the sum of three hundred pounds sells and conveys land on the Pigg River at the mouth of Hatchet Run and on both sides of the River, consisting of two entire tracts, one containing 67 acres and the other 187 acres, both patented by WILLIAM COOK and part of one patented to JOHN PHILPS and conveyed to COOK estimated to be 100 acres more or less, the three joining lines containing 354 acres with lines of: PETER HARDEMAN in PHILPSES old tract, EARLY and CALLAWAY. Signed: WILLIAM COOK.

Page 497. 24 July 1784. THOMAS JONES of the county of Henry to WILLIAM GRIFFY of the same for the sum of ten pounds sells and conveys land on both sides of Turner's Creek of Pigg River, being 107 acres and being part of a tract held by grant bearing date at Richmond of 1 September 1780. Signed: THOMAS JONES. Wit: WILLIAM MAVITY, P. HAIRSTON, ALEXANDER HUNTER, JOHN JONES.

Pages 498, 499. 3 May 1784. AMOS EVANS to CHARLES MATLOCK for the sum of thirty five pounds sells and conveys land on the south side of Smith River containing 22 acres, it being the land

EVANS bought of JOSEPH WEBSTER. Signed: AMOS EVANS. Wit: WILLIAM COGGIN, WILLIAM MATLOCK, RICHARD BAKER.

Pages 499, 500. 1 July 1784. JEREMIAH SHELTON of the county of Henry to CHARLES PIGG for the sum of thirty five pounds sells 154 acres of land on the north fork of Mayo River, it being the land granted to JEREMIAH SHELTON 1 September 1780. Signed: JEREMIAH SHELTON. Wit: A. HUGHES, JESSE ATKINSON, JOHN COLLEY.

Page 501. 13 April 1784. PHILLIP BLASSINGHAM and FRANCES BLASSINGHAM, his wife, to ALLEN BRACK for the sum of sixty pounds sells land containing by survey 50 acres more or less on the north side of Snow Creek joining THOMAS BOLTON. Signed: PHILLIP BLASSINGHAM (X), FRANCES (X) BLASSINGHAM. Wit: THOMAS DYER, DANIEL RICHARDSON, ABEL EDWARDS, JOHN DAVIS.

Pages 502, 503. 24 March 1784. JOHN NEWMAN and MARTHA his wife to HENRY KOGER for the sum of one hundred pounds sells land on Stone's Creek containing by estimate 218½ acres, joins lines of DANIEL NEWMAN. Signed: JOHN NEWMAN. Wit: ABRM. PENN, SAMUEL STAPLES, CHARLES HIBBERT.

Pages 503, 504. 27 May 1784. JOSHUA DILLINGHAM to SAMUEL BYRD for the sum of fifty pounds sells land on the waters of Chestnut Creek containing 185 acres more or less joins THOMAS WATTS. Signed: JOSHUA DILLINGHAM. Wit: WILLIAM RYAN, THOMAS PRUNTY, JOHN COX.

Page 505. 22 July 1784. EDMOND SWINNEY of the county of Henry to BENJAMIN MIZE for the sum of ten pounds sells land on both sides of Nicholases Creek containing 20 acres more or less. Signed: EDMUND SWINNEY.

Pages 506, 507. 20 March 1784. ROBERT GRIMMETT of the county of Henry to SAMUEL PATTERSON for the sum of thirty pounds sells land on the waters of Chestnut Creek containing 70 acres more or less. Signed: ROBERT (X) GRIMMETT. Wit: JOHN DICKERSON, WILLIAM WYNNE, JONATHAN DAVIS.

Page 508. 22 July 1784. EDWARD CHOAT, SR. of Henry County to CALLAWAY & EARLY for the sum of one hundred pounds sell one certain tract, parcel or piece of land in Henry County containing 290 acres as by patent bearing date 20 June MDCCLXXX with lines of

JOHN HOLLOWAY, JAMES SMITH. Signed: EDWARD (X) CHOAT.

Page 509. 16 July 1784. JOHN ARTHUR and SUSANNAH his wife of the county of Bedford to JACOB HICKMAN of the county of Henry for the sum of two hundred pounds sells a parcel of land containing 174 acres on Snake Run, a branch of Blackwater River, beginning at Daniel Run where JACOB BRILLIMON (PRILLIMAN) new line takes off. Signed: JOHN ARTHUR, SUSANA ARTHUR. Wit: DANIEL SPRANGLER, JOSEPH MILLER, T. ARTHUR, JOHN KELLY.

Pages 510, 511. 22 July 1784. JOSEPH GRAVELY of the county of Henry to NICHOLAS AKINS for the sum of three pounds grants to said NICHOLAS AKINS one tract or parcel of land in the county of Henry ajoining land where said AKINS now lives containing 25 acres more or less, beginning at a corner that divides GRAVELY and old AKIN tract. Signed: JOSEPH GRAVELY. Wit: LARKEN TARRENT.

Pages 511, 512. 22 July 1784. JOHN DICKENSON of the county of Henry to BARTLETT WADE for the sum of fifty pounds sells and conveys a parcel of land containing 379 acres on the south side of Pigg River, beginning at CHOATS corner post oak, HILL'S line, crosses a branch, GRIMMITT'S line. Signed: JOHN DICKINSON.

Page 513. 23 July 1784. JOSEPH BOWLING of the county of Henry to JOHN COX for the sum of twenty seven pounds ten shillings sells land on the head of Chestnut Creek, a branch of Town Creek, with line of JOHN DONELSON, crossing COLE'S Road and contains 264 acres. Signed: JOSEPH (X) BOLLING.

Page 514. 28 May 1784. Release of dower. LUCY MORTON, wife of JOHN MORTON releases her right of dower to a land transaction of 850 acres in Henry County.

Page 515. Bond. JOHN SALMON with JOHN COX as security, post bond as he is appointed coroner for Henry County.

Page 516. 22 July 1784. JAMES LYON of the county of Henry to JOHN FLETCHER for the sum of two pounds sells 36 acres of land on the west branch of Matthews Creek. Signed: JAMES LYON.

Page 517. 22 July 1784. JAMES LYON to JAMES MANKIN

for the sum of one hundred pounds sell land being 216 acres on the north side of Russells Creek. Signed: JAMES LYON.

Page 518. 17 November 1783. DAVY HALEY, JR. to HARRISON HOBART for the sum of one hundred pounds sells land on the south side of Smith River containing 50 acres. Signed: DAVID HALEY, JR. Wit: WILLIAM MATLOCK, JOHN PHILPOTT, SAMUEL PHILPOTT.

A list of surveys made of Henry County from June 10, 1779 to June 10, 1780 by JOHN DICKENSON and his associates.

For	Location	Acreage
WILLIAM RYAN	Snow Creek	202
JAMES PRUNTY	Snow Creek	232
LEWIS JENKINS	Turkey Creek	335
ROBERT PEDIGOW	Reed & Beaver Creek	362
JOHN KEEN	Pigg River	420
LANSFORD HALL	Waters Pigg River	202
ROBERT HODGES	Pigg River & Chestnut	193
JONATHAN DAVIS	Chestnut Creek	530
JOSEPH LYALL	Leatherwood Creek	206
JOSEPH LYALL	Turkey Cock	166
WILLIAM RYAN-	A survey altered	242
JARROTT BIRCH	Leatherwood Creek	412
SAMUEL JOHNSTON	Leatherwood Creek	308
Same	Same	410
GEORGE RUNNOLDS	Same	200
THOMAS CALLAWAY	Sandy River waters	400
FRANCIS COX	Leatherwood waters	278
GEORGE RUNNOLDS	Same	469
RUSSELL COX	Same	674
JOHN MITCHELL	Sandy River waters	379
WILLIAM SAMS & WATKINS	Cascade	411
JOSEPH GRAVLEY	Leatherwood	196
SAMUEL JOHNSTON	Same	350
JOHN COLLIAR	Same	336
ROBERT PEDIGOW	Leatherwood & Talbots Creek	1214
ROBERT PEDIGOW	Leatherwood	395
DANIEL MCBRIDE	Same	278
THOMAS COOPER	Same	450
PHILLIP THOMAS	Smith River	212
JOHN SIMMONS	Grassey Creek	638
JOHN SALMON	Wart Mountain	363
WILLIAM HALBERT	Russells Creek	486
JAMES MANKIN	Same	290

RICHARD DICKONS	Same	353
HENRY PARR	Mayo River	445
WILLIAM WILSON	Spoon River	411
ABRAHAM FRAZIER	Same	266
PHILLIP BUZZARD	Same	383
JOHN MARR	Same	350
JOHN GRISHAM	Same	344
WILLIAM POOR	Same	391
JAMES DICKENSON	Same	361
SAMUEL ALLEN	Goblingtown Creek	174
JOHN FARRELL	Sycamore Creek	595
Same	Same	155
RICHARD KIRBY	Sycamore Creek	358
WILLIAM ISHAM	Same	271
THOMAS MORRISON	Same	180
JOHN NEVELLS	Same	334
WILLIAM AMOSE	Same	491
WILLIAM JONES	Same	261
RICHARD RUNNOLDS	Smith River	312
ANTHONY TITTLE	Goblintown Creek	415
WILLIAM BIRKS	Same	133
CHARLES FOSTER	Smith River	260
ELECTUSOUS MUSICK	Goblintown Creek	240
WILLIAM HANKINS	Turkey Cock	838
DANIEL HANKINS	Same	316
Same	Same	225
JOHN DICKINSON	Leatherwood	980
SAMUEL JOHNSTON	Same	272
ROBERT WATSON	Same	252
JAMES EAST	Horsepasture	286
Same	Same	178
RICHARD WELCH	Stone's Creek	147
JACOB COGER	Same	117
DANIEL NEWMAN	Same	442
Same	Same	205
JOHN F. MILLER	Mayo River	464
Same	Same	205
JOHN WATSON	Horsepasture Creek	464
JOHN NEWMAN	Stone's Creek	182
BARTLETT RUNNOLDS	Same	367
RICHARD ADAMS	Mill Creek	434
THOMAS ADAMS	Same	428
ARCHELEUS HUGHES	Same	315
JESSE RUNNOLDS	Stone's Creek	256
THOMAS LOCKHART	Mayo waters	453
NEHEMIAH PRAYTHOR	Mayo waters	160
JOHN COGAR	Same	386
JOSIAH SMITH	Same	343
JOHN CAMERON	Same	213
MOSES RUNNOLDS	Same	157
RICHARD DICKONS	Grays fork	594
JAMES TAYLOR	Mayo River	422
SAMUEL PARKER	Same	167
JOHN BARKER	Spoon River	458
JOSIAH SMITH	Stone's Creek	302
JONATHAN HANBY	Peters Creek	880
WOODY BURGE	Elk Creek	325
AUGUSTINE BROWN	Peters Creek	680
ISAAC CLOUD	Elk Creek	167
DAVID ROGERS	Peters Creek	182
WILLIAM SMITH	Same	330
HENRY DILLIAN	Storuds Creek	535
SHADRACK TURNER	Town Creek	306
JOSIAH TURNER	Same	326
WILLIAM HUNTER	Same	182
DANIEL SMITH	Same	232
JOHN BIBEY	Daniels Run	103
HENRY WILLIS	on Blue Ridge	164
JOHN WILLIS	Coles Creek	628
GEORGE HAIRSTON	Smith River	467

Name	Water	Acres
Same	waters Smith River	442
LUKE THORNTON	Chestnut Creek	237
WILLIAM WARRAIN	Same	313
JOHN WOOD	Same	350
MILES JENNINGS	Mayo River	474
GEORGE TAYLOR	Mayo Waters	254
HENRY FEE	Same	152
JOHN SIMS	Same	172
JESSE ATKERSON	Same	280
A. HUGHES	Same	304
JAMES SHARD	Same	432
ROBERT BAKER	Same	155
Same	Same	205
RICHARD ADAMS	Green Creek	377
JOHN PARR, SR.	Mayo River	391
Same	Same	374
JOHN LYON	Russell Creek	153
SHADRACK TURNER	Wedgion Creek	254
JESSE HELTON	Jack's Creek	336
CHARLES THOMAS	Poplar Camp Creek	492
PALETIAH SHELTON	Wedgion Creek	251
CHARLES THOMAS	Joint Crack Creek	394
SAMUEL ALLEN	Jack's Creek	112
ISAAC MCDANIEL	Dan River	900
SAMUEL HELTON	Turnip Creek	364
JOHN DICKENSON	Leatherwood Creek	257
Same	Same	180
PATRICK HENRY	Smith R. & Leatherwood	949
GARROTT MORE	Leatherwood	238
JOHN FONTAINE	Leatherwood	238
JOHN ACUFF	Same	197
ABRAHAM PARSELY	Beaver Creek	124
PETER COPLAND	Beaver waters	407
RALPH ELKINS	Same	206
ABRAHAM PARSLEY	Beaver &' Reed Crk waters	265
PETER COPLAND	Beaver waters	310
GEORGE HAIRSTON & CO.	waters Smith River	584
PETER COPLAND	Reed Creek	356
JOHN ROWLAND	Same	412
HENRY SUMPTER	Rock Run	1494
HENRY BARKSDALE	Same	142
ANTHONY SMITH	Mayo waters	440
JOHN WILLINGHAM	....	56
HENRY TATE	Smith River	172
BAYNES CARTER	Smith River waters	201
JOSIAH SMITH	Horsepasture Crk	189
DUTTON LAYNE	Same	642
JAMES EAST	Same	670
WILLIAM TAYLOR	Same	85
JOHN RICHARDSON	Same	259
JOHN WILDRAKE BENDERSHIRE	Stones Creek	56
JOHN BLEVINS	Horsepasture Crk	277
THOMAS JAMESON	Marrowbone Crk	315
HOWELL IVIE	Matrimony Crk	215
WILLIAM SAMS	Same	223
JOHN STEPHENS	Home Creek	236
JAMES OLDHAM	Home Creek	268
JAMES EDWARDS	Smith River	102
DAVID ROGERS	Russell Crk	378
THOMAS WILLIS	Same	339
AUGUSTIN BROWN	Peters Creek	162
DAVID LAWSON	Hics. fork	598
JOHN PARR, JR.	Russell Creek	241
JAMES LYON	Same	400
JOSHUA HUDSON	Same	355
WILLIAM LYNCH	Mayo River	295
JOEL BARKER	Same	288
SAMUEL COX	Dan River	400
BENJAMIN GARROTT	Same	400

Name	Location	Acres
JOHN DANIEL	Same	300
JOHN GLASSUP	Suns Run	106
DANIEL RICE	Stone's Creek	231
WILLIAM VESS	Mayo River	175
THOMAS STOCKTON	Same	302
WILLIAM MEAD & Co.	Dan River	1586
AZARIAH SHELTON	Mayo River	971
JAMES LYON	Same	300
JOHN SHELTON	Same	889
THOMAS GAZAWAY	Same	401
GEORGE POOR	Furys fork	351
HENRY SMITH	Russell Creek	207
JOHN RICHARDSON	Mayo River	256
BARTLETT SIMS	Same	531
ELIAPHAS SHELTON	Same	365
BLACKMORE HUGHES	Smith River	687
JOHN PARR, SR.	Mayo River	148
JAMES MCBRIDE	Jack's Creek	422
JAMES ELKINS	Grassey Creek	168
THOMAS HENDERSON	Smith River	336
JOHN ISON, SR.	Same	118
EDWARD PEDIGOW	Grassey Creek	50
JOHN RATLIFF	Smith River	60
ISAAC MCDANIEL	Rockcastle Creek	70
JOHN SMALL	Jill's Creek	164
JAMES ELKINS	Smith River	442
DAVID HARBOUR	Sycamore	134
CHARLES BARNARD	Same	360
RICHARD KERBY	Same	111
ABNOR BARNARD	Same	206
LUKE FOLEY	Same	629
NATHAN HALL	Smith River	465
JOHN HANDY	Beardy Creek	188
ROBERT STOCKTON	Same	192
ROBERT HAIRSTON	Runnett Bagg	132
Same	Same	774
WILLIAM RENTFROW	Same	145
ROBERT STOCKTON	Nicholas' Creek	286
Same	Same	662
JOHN OBRIAN	Same	178
ROBERT STOCKTON	Same	52
SAMUEL HAIRSTON	Same	1044
NATHANIEL DIXON	Same	206
DANIEL PRILLEYMAN	Same	285
WILLIAM FARGUSON	Same	725
JOHN KEELE	Same	444
SAMUEL PACKWOOD	Mill Creek	273
SAMUEL HAIRSTON	Nicholas Creek	236
JOSEPH DAVIS	Same	566
JESSE CHANDLER	Marrowbone Creek	114
JOHN RICHARDSON	Same	129
ANDREW REA	Grassey Creek	102
JESSE WILLINGHAM	Marrowbone Creek	135
ARMSTEAD ANDERSON	Same	219
JOHN HARDMAN	Same	253
JAMES MAY	Matrimony Creek	460
THOMAS EDWARDS	Smith River	550
JOHN KELLY	Same	254
THOMAS CHOWNING	Same	470
JOHN WIMBISH	Same	285
JOHN MORGAN	Same	310
JAMES COX	Same	425
DANIEL WILSON	Same	336
JAMES COX	Middle Creek	293
THOMAS PARSLEY	Marrowbone Creek	289
JOHN REA	Smith River	700
JOHN BURNS	Marrowbone	183
GEORGE F. HARRIS	Home Creek	191
Same	Cascade	78
GRIMES HOLCOMB	Town Creek	109
JOHN YOUNG	Stones Creek	309

HUGH MCWILLIAMS	Reedy Creek	443	
BENJAMIN HENSLEY	Same	288	
JOHN DICKINSON	Pigg River	219	
SOLOMAN DAVIS	Same	202	
ISHAM HODGES	Same	249	
ROBERT HOOKER	Stone's Creek	309	

A list of surveys made from June 10, 1780 to June 10, 1783.

FOR	ACREAGE	FOR	ACREAGE
JOHN HENDERSON	122	THOMAS VAUGHAN	300
THOMAS MILLER	36	HUGH WOODS	126
STEPHEN LEE	134	AUGUSTINE BROWN	320
WILLIAM KELLEY	158	WOODY BURGE	128
JOSEPH LEWIS	257	JOHN WATSON	190
Same	174	RICHARD BAKER	218
HENRY TATE	200	JONATHAN HANBY	110
GEORGE HAIRSTON	400	JOHN WATSON	400
JESSE CLOUD	380	JOHN HENDERSON	70
JACOB ADAMS	195	THOMAS MILLER	126
JOHN PHELPREY	176	THOMAS COX	75
WILLIAM REED	259	JESSE WILSON	103
Same	270	PETER STUMP	100
HENRY DILLIN	372	JOHN MARR	34
BENJAMIN DILLIN	315	JAMES LYON	222
BAYNES CARTER	148	ISAAC CLOUD & Co.	313
JOHN BARROTT	262	JOHN MARR	221
CARTER & JINNINGS	528	Same	400
SAMUEL STREET	298	ABRAHAM EDES	344
ISAAC CLOUD	113	HUDSPETH & C.	465
GEORGE ROGARS	242	GEORGE ALLEN	126
WOODY BURGE	43	MUNFORD SMITH	70
ELIPHAZ SHELTON	590	JOHN HAMMONS	202
WILLIAM CLOUD	196	WILLIAM MANN	114,300
WILLIAM WOODS	225	ELIPHAZ SHELTON	72
GEORGE CARTER	317	CORNELIUS KEETH	130,133
PALITIAH SHELTON	90	WILLIAM WEBB	108
ESTATE OF JAMES SMIS	47	GEORGE EVANS	300
WILLIAM ARNOLD	133	JAMES CHARLES	155
WILLIAM WEATHERSPOON	249	ISHAM WEBB	170
Same	64	SKEEFAND DONELSON	117
GEORGE CARTER	211	AUGUSTINE BROWN	330
HAYMAN CRITZ, JR.	43	KEEFAND DONELSON	218
GEORGE CARTER	305	RICHARD BENNETT	168
HAMON CRITZ, JR.	371	BENJAMIN HENSLEY	80
Same	200	THOMAS MEDKIFF	160
Same	210	WILLIAM SMITH	1178
ISHAM HODGES	193	HAYMON FRANCE	328
SAMUEL PATTERSON	235	THOMAS SMITH	329
WILLIAM JAMESON	325	JOHN SHELTON	174
Same	311	GEORGE POOR	90,198
WILLIAM DILLINGHAM	323	BENJAMIN CUMMINGS	364
DANIEL JONES	165	JAMES TAYLOR	445
THOMAS HEARD	100	JAMES ECTON	321
RICHARD PERRYMAN	400	ABRAHAM ADAMS	262
Same	340	MARVEL NASH	445
STEPHEN HEARD	106,293,397,303	JOHN RANDOLPH	219,291
JOHN HARTWELL	321	JAMES PIGG	200
JESSE HEARD	413	JOHN PULLAM	174
JAMES EDMUNDSON	180	ESTATE;JAMES CAMERON	349
EDWARD CHOAT	307	JACOB CAYTON	560
JOHN GOWIN	374	GEORGE DANIEL	126
Same	79	EDWARD COCKERAM	165
HENRY SUMPTER	311	JAMES ARMSTRONG	169
JOHN WITT	222	JACOB MCCRAW	111,300
JOHN GOSSETT	446	JAMES ARMSTRONG	32
PETER RICKMAN	351	JAMES HARRINGTON	250
ISRAEL STANDEFER	419	THOMAS CARLING	86
JOHN PHILPOTT	241	JOSEPH PAXTON	192

Name	Acres
WILLIAM WEBB	206
MOSES JOHNSON	400
THOMAS HILL	462
JOHN STEWART	50
NICHOLUS BAKER & C.	400,800
HENRY PARR	395
DANIEL CARLAND	84,250,381
JOHN KELLEY	200
JOHN MARR	300
LADOCK SMITH	338
STEPHEN HEARD	269,460
GEORGE STULTS	96
RICHARD COLLIER	292
ARCH. HUGHES	270,400
JAMES BARTLETT	266
JOHN PULLOM	213
PETER RICKMAN	249
GEORGE EVANS	30
WILLIAM WOODS	450
SOLOMON HELTON	190
EDWARD TAYTOM (TATUM)	106
STEPHEN SENTER	300
GEORGE WATKINS	37
WILLIAM MAVITY	223
JOSEPH DAVIS	536
DAVID BARTON	443
THOMAS JONES	275
JOSEPH DAVIS	179
THOMAS JONES	162
JESSE BROCK	188
JOHN DICKENSON	396
JAMES PRUNTY	162
JOHN NAIL (NEAL)	309
SAMUEL BAIRD (BYRD)	149
THOMAS BOULDIN	212
THOMAS BOULDIN	200
WILLIAM THARP	102,157
GIDEON SMITH	455
WALTER MCCOY	96
DARBY RYAN	146
BAILEY CARTER	100
OBID BAKER	550,680
ISAAC CLOUD	101
ARTHUR EDWARDS	200
TALBOTT & MEAD	88
FARGUSON & MAVITY	1456
WILLIAM HARRIS	111
SAMUEL PATTERSON	345
JOHN NEVILLS	231
EDWARD BAKER	256
JOHN BUTLER	263
MARTIN & HORD	190
ESTATE; B. MUSGROVE	100
JOHN HAYS	90
ROBERT PEDEGOW	776
SHAREWOOD BIBY	70
BENJAMIN HALE	190
WILLIAM KELLEY	60
JOHN HENDERSON	46,172
JOHN MINTER	384,441
JOHN HICKEY	102,450
RICHARD T. MAYNOR	370
GEORGE SUMPTER	40
EDWARD SWINNEY	346
ROBERT PEDEGOW	292,236
JAMES CASEY	209
JOHN BARKER	181
WILLIAM SHARP	90
THOMAS MURROUGH	86
PATRICK HENRY	2125
ABIRT MEAD	228
DAVID GOWEN	94
RICHARD HOLT	435
MOSES RUNNOLDS	202
THOMAS FLOWERS	122
ROBERT PENSEY(?)	174
ROBERT PERRYMAN	226
WILLIAM FARGUSON	208
AUGUSTINE CHOAT	202
JACOB PRILLEYMAN	65
THOMAS JONES, JR.	400
ROBERT JONES	160
LYON & CLOUD	300
WILLIAM DAVIS	148
JOHN HICKEY	155
JOHN RENFROW	302

* Deed pgs 473, 474
28 May 1784
THOMAS MATHEWS to ZAPHANIAH WADE of the county of Henry for the sum of one hundred pounds sells and conveys land on Little Beaver Creek containing 70 acres, joins lines of JOHN HOLMNS, WILLIAM WHITSITTS, PETER COPLAND.

THOMAS MATHEWS

INDEX

Names which have been underlined appeared in original Index,
but cannot be located on page indicated.

ABINGTON
    Bowles, 35, 81, 82, 100
    John, 35
    John, Sr., 99
    Lucy, 35

ACUFF
    John, 50, 75, 81, 87, 108
    William, 67

ADAMS
    Abraham, 24, 110
    Jacob, 38, 72, 110
    Richard, 107, 108
    Thomas, 107
    William, 38

ADKINSON
    Joel, 8

AGEE
    Mathew, 60

AKIN
    Joseph, 5
    Nicholas, 34, 105

ALEE
    Nicholes, 3

ALEXANDER
    John, 48, 57, 74, 81, 83
    John, Jr., 5, 25
    William, 6, 7, 36, 58

ALLEN
    Samuel, 97, 107, 108
    George, 110

ALLSOP, ALLSUP
    Joseph, 41, 79

AMOSE
    William, 107

ANDERSON
    Armstead, 109

ANGLIN
    Phillip, 7

ANTHONY
    James, 8, 9, 11, 40, 41, 46, 91,
        93, 102
    Joseph, 12, 32, 82, 91, 93, 101,
        102
    Micajah, 39

ARDON
    Abraham, 97

ARMSTRONG
    Hugh, 5, 10, 24
    James, 24, 110

ARNOLD
    Henry, 92
    William, 110

ARSKIN
    Henry, 78
    Jean, 78

ARTHUR
    John, 29, 33, 105
    Susannah, 105
    T., 105
    Thomas, 64

ATKINS
    Jacob, 44

ATKERSON, ATKINSON
    Jesse, 104, 108

BAILEY
    Carr, 36, 38
    Martha, 97

BAIRD, See BYRD
    Jonathan, 91

BAKER
    Edward, 71, 111
    James, 60, 87
    John, 111
    Joseph, 9
    Nicholus & C., 111
    Obid, 111
    Richard, 104, 111
    Robert, 7, 80, 85, 90, 102, 108

BANKS
    John, 13, 14

BARBERRY, BARBERYES
    James, 68, 75

BARKER
    Charles, 38
    Edward, 38
    Joel, 96, 108
    John, 21, 92, 97, 106
    John, Sr., 98

BARKSDALE, BARKSDILL
    Henry, 34, 45, 71, 85
    John, 40, 41, 45, 54, 60, 66, 71,
        75, 84, 85, 89, 93, 108

BARSDILL
    John, 93

BARNARD
    Abnor, 109
    Charles, 109

BARNETT
    Nathan, 18

BARROTT
  John, 110
BARTEE
  Mary, 95
  William, 48, 91, 95
BARTLETT
  James, 71, 111
BARTON
  David, 111
  Isaac, 23, 57, 63
  William, 21
BATES
  Isaac, 66, 85
  James, 9
BAYS
  Peter, 82, 90
BAUGHAN
  Aris, 52
BEAZLEY
  Charles, 86
BECK
  Paul, 28, 44
BEDFORD
  Thomas, 54, 56, 61, 88
BELCHER
  Isam, 86
BELL
  William, 66
BENDER
  John, 61
BENDERSHIRE
  John Wildrake, 108
BENNETT
  Bimberey, 3
  Richard, 110
BERRY
  Thomas, 72
BEVINS
  Charles, 36
  Samuel, 36
BIBEY, BIBY
  John, 107
  Sharwood, 111
BILLINGS
  Anthony, 22
BINNON
  Martin, 95
BIRCH, See BURCH

BIRK
  Rowland Horsley, 82, 90
  William, 107
BITTING, BITTEN
  Anthony, 8, 15, 36, 55, 75, 91, 93
BLACK
  Thomas, 43
  William, 11, 20, 22
BLAGG, BLAGGE
  John, 15, 16
BLAIN
  John, 74
BLAKEY
  Churchill, 81
BLANKENSHIP
  Elijah, 80
  Hezekiah, 75
  Isham, 76, 80
  William, 51
BLASSINGAME, BLESSINGAME, BLASHINGHAM
  Frances, 104
  Phillip, 33, 43, 47, 104
BLEVINS
  Agnes, 48, 49
  Dillion, 17, 27, 40, 41
  John, 2, 4, 8, 23, 94, 108
  William, 4, 9, 49
  William, Jr., 4
  William, Sr., 2, 94
BLOGGE
  John, 92
BOHANNON
  John, 14, 33
  William, 44
BOLLING, BOLING, BOWLING
  Abi, 47
  Archibald, 50
  George, 12
  Jane, 50
  John, 6, 12
  Joseph, 105
  Rebeccah, 12
  Samuel, 17, 47, 70, 79
BOLTON, BOULTON
  Ann, 18, 34, 50
  Elizabeth, 50
  James, 18,
  Man, 18
  Mary, 18, 34, 56
  Robert, 5, 18, 19, 33, 34, 56, 80, 99
  Robert, Jr., 5, 50
  Thomas, 8, 17, 47, 81, 104
BOOTH
  John, 29

BOTTOM
  Thomas, 54

BOULDIN
  Joseph, 6, 7, 58
  Thomas, 6, 7, 58, 83, 111
  Thomas, Sr., 7

BOWLING, See BOLLING

BOYD
  William, 89

BRACK
  Allen, 104

BRAMER
  James, 102

BRASIER
  David, 86

BREEDING
  Frances, 3
  Richard, 3

BRETHEART, BRETHEAD
  William, 93, 94

BRILLIMON
  Jacob, 105

BRISCOE
  John, 67

BRISTOW
  John, 83

BRITTAIN
  George, 62

BROCK
  Jesse, 111
  Josiah, 34

BROSHEARS
  Phillip, 6, 81

BROWN
  Augustine, 106, 108, 111
  William, 33, 50, 75

BULLOCK
  Thomas, 13

BURCH, See also BIRCH
  Gerard, 41
  Jared, 29, 81, 106
  John, 29

BURDETT, BURDITT
  Humphrey, 46
  Jarvass, 46
  William, 46

BURGE
  Woody, 107, 110

BURGIS
  John, 65

BURNETT
  Catherine, 79
  Charles, 79

BURNS
  John, 109
  Mary Ann, 6
  Samuel, 6

BURTON
  Seth, 28

BUSH
  Thomas, 48, 56, 100

BUTLER
  John, 111

BUZZARD
  Phillip, 107

BYRD, BIRD, See also BAIRD
  Francis, 38
  Mary, 24
  Samuel, 24, 66, 104, 111

CALDWELL
  David, 26

CALLAND
  Samuel, 98

CALLAWAY
  James, 38, 43, 64, 99
  Thomas, 106

CALLAWAY & EARLY, 104

CAMERON, CAMRON
  James, 110
  John, 38, 56, 107
  Joseph, 16

CAMPBELL, CAMBRIL
  Hugh, 22, 42
  Thomas, 72
  William, 39

CAMREAL
  John,

CANTRELL
  Joshua, 102

CARGILL
  James, 11

CARLAND, CARLIN
  Daniel, 17, 111

CARLING
  Thomas, 110

CARTER & JINNINGS, 110

CARTER
  Bailey, 74, 87, 88, 89, 90, 111
  Baynes, 20, 42, 60, 66, 92, 100, 103, 108, 110
  George, 11, 92

CARTER, Cont'd.
John, 90
Joseph, 88, 90
Josiah, 9, 20, 21, 53, 55, 60, 75, 92
Josias, 9
Martha, 103
Mary, 92
Nancy, 21
Thomas, 43
William, 92

CASEY
James, 111

CATON
Joseph, 29

CAVE
Robert, 52

CAYTON
Jacob, 110

CHADWELL
David, 24, 38, 73
Elizabeth, 24

CHANDLER
Benjamin, 31, 69
Jesse, 31, 33, 109
Joseph, 32
Pertheney, 10
Robert, 9, 10, 32, 84

CHARLES
James, 110

CHILDRESS
Eona, 91
John, 4

CHILES
Nancy, 57
Rowland, 57, 90, 100

CHOICE
Ann, 26
Tully, 26, 30, 47, 68, 70, 97
Tully, Jr., 26
William, 70, 84

CHOAT, CHOATES
Augustine, 111
Christopher, 83
Edward, 91, 92, 105, 110
Edward, Sr., 104
Sabrot, 101

CHOWNING
Thomas, 77, 79, 109

CHUST
Henry, 26

CLACK
Spencer, 10, 11, 15, 16, 40, 41, 68

CLARK, CLARKE
Henry, 91, 102
Samuel, 80, 85, 86

CLAUNCHE
Jeremiah, 100

CLAY
Jesse, 43, 86, 87, 91
Miriam, 86
William, 28, 77

CLEMENT
Mathew, 58

CLOUD
Isaac, 107, 110, 111
Jesse, 110
Joseph, 10
William, 110

CLORE, CLOWER
Jacob, 85
Mical, 62

COCKERHAM
Abner, 17
Edward, 110

COGER, See KOGER

COGGIN
William, 24, 104

COHAN
Jacob, 60

COCKRAN
Abner, 99
William, 75, 86

COLE
Walter King, 74, 86, 101, 102

COLEMAN
John, 9
Williamson, 29

COLLIER, COLLYER, COLYAR
John, 24, 106
Richard, 23, 88, 111

CONWAY, CONNAWAY, CONNWAY
also McCONWAY
Betsy, 100
John, 40, 41, 67, 79, 81, 87, 100
Mary, 67

COOK
Benjamin, 10, 26, 58, 68, 79, 97
Benjamin, Jr., 26, 38
Benjamin, Sr., 26, 38
James, 16
Joseph, 79
Mary, 38
Shem, 10
Shim, 51
William, 2, 14, 32, 34, 43, 47, 88, 103

COLLEY, COOLEY
  Ann, 85
  James, 43, 84, 85
  John, 104

COOPER
  John, 8, 11, 15, 22, 55, 74, 75, 82
  Joseph, 8, 21, 36, 37, 39, 68, 94
  Thomas, 8, 19, 24, 36, 39, 41, 46, 54, 68, 74, 75, 94, 106
  Thomas, Jr., 8, 9
  Thomas, Sr., 9

COPLAND
  Charles, 5, 8, 11, 15
  Elizabeth, 11, 16, 19, 20, 21, 22, 24, 36, 58
  Peter, 4, 8, 9, 11, 12, 15, 16, 17, 19, 20, 21, 22, 23, 24, 25, 36, 37, 38, 39, 46, 50, 51, 52, 54, 58, 59, 60, 74, 75, 100, 103, 108
  Richard, 15, 51
  Sally, 8, 11, 15, 36

CORNWELL
  William, 62, 78

COURSEY
  James, 46

COUTHS, COUTTS
  Patrick, 4, 9, 41

COWDEN
  James, 3, 17, 28, 34, 79
  William, 4, 79, 91

COX
  Francis, 3, 21, 34, 81, 90, 106
  George, 14
  George, Jr., 14, 15
  Jacob, 17
  James, 13, 14, 15, 66. 108
  James, Jr., 13, 66
  James, Sr., 13, 66
  Jemimah, 36
  John, 1, 4, 5, 12, 15, 16, 17, 31, 32, 38, 41, 49, 59, 63, 66, 70, 71, 72, 74, 83, 90, 93, 94, 104, 105
  Mary, 12, 14, 15
  Robert, 38
  Russell, 6, 106
  Samuel, 108
  Thomas, 90, 110
  Tolivar, 6
  William, 36

CREWS
  Thomas, 61

CRIST
  Elizabeth, 29
  Henry, 29
  Jacob, 29

CRITZ
  Hamon, 37, 62, 63, 90
  Hamon, Jr., 110
  Hamon, Sr., 42

CROUCH
  John, 21, 52
  Joseph, 52

CRUNK
  Hannah, 24

CUMMINGS
  Benjamin, 110
  Malachiah, 38, 72
  Thomas, 77

CUNNINGHAM
  John, 37, 52, 75, 76
  John, Jr., 6

CUTCHAM
  James, 102

DANDRIDGE
  William, 50

DANIEL, DANIELD
  George, 46, 110
  John, 17, 65, 108
  John, Sr., 17, 22
  Mary, 64
  Robert, 36
  Sarah, 22, 65

DARNALL
  Nicholas, 79
  Susanna, 79

DAVIS
  John, 34, 40, 43, 90, 104
  Jonathan, 104, 106
  Joseph, 87, 108, 111
  Soloman, 14, 26, 43, 110
  William, 44, 111
  Zacheriah, 101

DAY
  John, 97

DEAKINS, See DICKENS

DEATHERAGE
  George, 10

DELANHAM
  William, 85

DEPRIEST
  Tabitha, 64

DEWASE
  Lewis, 74

DICKENSON
  James, 7, 80, 85, 90, 105, 107
  John, 2, 16, 43, 56, 77, 89, 104, 107, 108, 110, 111
  Obediah, 83

DICKERSON
  John, 21, 22, 38, 42, 44, 62, 66, 79
  Obediah, 102
  Thomas, 79
  Thompson, 66, 79

DICKENS, DICKONS
  Mary, 82
  Richard, 82, 84, 107

DICKSON, See DIXON
  Nathaniel, 74

DILLARD
  John, 42, 45, 51, 61, 62, 63, 71, 76

DILLEN, DILLIN, DILLON
  Benjamin, 37, 110
  Henry, 107, 110
  James, 80

DILLINGHAM, DYLINGHAM also see WILLINGHAM
  Jesse, 93, 94
  John, 87
  Joshua, 104
  Michael, 21, 60, 71
  William, 79, 110

DIXON, See also DICKSON
  Nathaniel, 109

DOAKE, DOOKE
  James, 4, 10

DOBBS
  Foster, 59
  John, 59

DOGGET
  Miller, 32, 74
  Milton, 44
  Richard, 3

DOIGHTER
  John, 64

DONALD
  James, 75
  Robert, 6, 17, 75, 91, 92, 100

DONELSON
  Alexander, 39
  John, 38
  Rachel, 38
  Skeefand, 110

DOOLEY
  Thomas, 9

DUNCAN
  James, 24
  John, 10

DUNLAP
  Henry, 12, 21

DUNN
  Michael, 43,
  Waters, 41, 60
  Waters, Jr., 33
  William, 44, 71, 88

DURHAM
  Gregory, 45, 88

DUVALL
  Benjamin, 76
  Lewis, 76

DYER
  Thomas, 104

EARLS
  Thomas, 66

EARLY
  Jeremiah, 38, 64, 69
  John, 43, 64
  Joseph, 43, 64
  Jubal, 64
  Mary, 64

EARLY & CALLAWAY, 43, 103, 104

EASSON
  Francis, 85

EAST
  Elphan, 82
  James, 26, 64, 96, 107, 108
  James, Sr., 82
  John, 32, 81, 83
  Joseph, 12, 32
  William, 18, 83

EASTES, See ESTES

ECTON
  James, 110

EDES
  Abraham, 110

EDMUNDSON
  James, 86, 110
  Richard, 46, 50, 68

EDWARDS
  Ann, 15
  Abel, 84, 104
  Arthur, 18, 78, 111
  Edmund, 22
  Elizabeth, 102
  James, 6, 68, 73, 102, 108
  Thomas, 6, 68, 81, 108
  William, Sr.
  William, 14, 15, 68, 102

EGGERS
  Daniel, 91

ELKINS
  James, 109
  Ralph, 108

ELLIOTT
George, 8, 9, 11

ELLIS
John, 8, 42
Joseph, 3
William, 5

ELLISON
Robert, 81

ERSKSRIDGE
Burdett, 12

EASTES, ESTES
Bottom, 48, 98, 101, 102
Elisha, Jr., 19
Elisha, Sr., 19, 33, 48, 68, 72
Frances, 19, 48
Joel, 40, 41, 60, 68, 71
Mary, 68
William, 26, 37, 46, 47, 52

EVANS
Amos, 78, 103, 104
Geo. 110, 111

FARGUSON, FERGUSON
Andrew, 65, 66
Catheron, 66
John, 35, 43, 63, 101
Joseph, 33
Patience, 33
R. , 12
Seph., 33
William, 44, 47, 101, 108, 111

FARGUSON & MAVITY, 111

FARRELL
John, 107

FARIS, FERRIS
Jacob, 101, 102

FEE
Henry, 108

FENCH
William, 78

FEWEL
William, 93

FINCH
Charles, 20
Joyce, 20

FINNEY
Thomas, 57

FITZGERALD
Frederick, 3

FITZPATRICK
Joseph, 51

FLETCHER
Ambrose, 4
Hannah, 4
John, 22, 105

FOLEY
Bartlett, 100
Luke, 74, 109

FLOWERS
Thomas, 37, 111

FONTAINE
John, 55, 58, 63, 81, 83, 94, 108

FONTON
Aaron, 43
Abraham, 43

FORD
Daniel, 73, 78, 93, 94
David, 73
Mary, 73
Molly, 93

FOSTER
Ann, 71
Charles, 71, 72, 107
Mark, 71, 72, 91
Mary, 71

FOX
Mary, 83
Samuel, 83

FRANCE
Haymon, 110
Henry, 7, 19, 96, 97, 99

FRANCISCO
Peter, 86

FRANKLING
Abraham Alexander, 36

FRAZIER, FRAZIER
Abraham, 107
Simon, 65

FREEMAN
Holman, 88

FRENCH
William, 62, 63, 93, 100

FULKERSON
Frederick, 19, 86
James, 65

GALIHORN
Asias, 67

GARDNER, GARDWIN
Henson, 59, 60
William, 37, 58, 59

GARNER
Thomas, 8, 11, 41

GARROTT
Benjamin, 108

GATES
James, 10
Samuel, 58

GATEWOOD
Ann Frazier, 33

GAZAWAY
Thomas, 109

GEARHEART
Leonard, 47
Lewis, 44
Peter, 44, 47

GEORGE
John, 32

GILLEY
Francis, 6

GILLIAM, GILLUM
Deverix, 26, 98, 99
Ede, (Edy), 26, 98
Peter, 43, 89

GLASSUP
John, 109

GODLARD
James, 24

GOLEHORN
John, 79

GOOD
John, 20

GOODWIN
Joseph, 25, 37

GOOLSBY
Daniel, 81

GOSSETT
John, 110.

GOUGE
Jane, 69,
Nathan, 69
Rachel, 68, 69

GOWEN
David, 111

GOWIN
John, 110

GRAVELY
Joseph, 13, 21, 34, 36, 81, 105, 106

GRAVES
William, 17, 18, 29, 48
William, Jr., 14
William, Sr., 14

GRAVITT
Obedah, 59

GRAY
Edmund, 5, 18, 27, 48,
William, 102

GRIMMETT, GRIMMITT
John, 14, 28
Robert, 104

GRIGGORY
John, 83

GRISHAM, GRESHAM
Barbury, 80
John, 6, 80, 85, 90, 107
John, Jr., 85

GWILLIAMS, See also WILLIAMS
Edgecomb, 10, 53, 61

GREEN
Philmer, 77, 93

GREER
James, 62, 73
William, 90

GRIFFY
William, 103

HAILE
Nicholas, 80

HAIRSTON
George, 2, 3, 15, 16, 20, 23, 25, 27, 31, 33, 35, 40, 41, 42, 46, 49, 50, 56, 61, 67, 72, 73, 81, 87, 89, 94, 95, 96, 100, 103, 107, 108, 110
George & Co., 108
P., 55, 57, 72, 103
Peter, 61, 100
Robert, 1, 67, 72, 92, 109
Samuel, 27, 55, 109,

HALBERT, See HOLBART

HALE
Benjamin, 111
George, 70
Jane, 72
Joseph, 27, 28, 85
Reachal, 28
Thomas, 21, 33, 34, 43, 72, 74, 85

HALEY, HALY, HAILEY
David, 5, 23, 36, 89, 90
David, Jr., 24, 106
David, Sr., 24
Ester, 89
John, 75, 82

HALL
Ambrose
Jesse, 77
John, 65
Lansford, 106
Million, 25
Nathan, 6, 18, 52, 90, 108
Randolph, 44, 51
Samuel, 25
William, 28, 29, 47, 93

HALKUM
  Grimes, 52

HAMILTON, HAMBLETON
  George, 15, 16, 22, 32, 33, 93
  Mary, 33, 55
  Thomas, 10, 26, 27, 31, 35, 46, 54

HAMMITT
  William, 78

HAMMON
  John, 110
  Thomas, 91
  William, 18

HAMMOND
  Salley, 50
  William, 18, 50

HAMPTON
  John, Major, 81
  Mary, 95
  Robert, 78, 95

HANBY
  David, 53
  Jonathan, 1, 17, 53, 59, 107, 110
  Sarah, 59

HANDY
  John, 109

HANES
  Jonathan, 71

HANKINS
  Daniel, 6, 7, 29, 107
  William, 107

HARBOUR
  Abner, 4, 7
  David, 7, 109
  Esaias, 84, 92
  Joel, 83, 92
  Sarah, 7
  Thomas, 7

HARDAIN
  Electious, 14
  Luke, 29

HARDEWAY
  Stanfield, 29

HARDMAN
  Charles, 12, 73, 78
  Elizabeth, 1, 96
  Faney, 12
  John, 1, 40, 41, 72, 73, 77, 78, 93, 94, 96, 108
  Peter, 103
  Uriah, 1, 12, 94
  William, 1, 30

HARGER
  John, 43

HARMER
  George, 101, 102
  John, 40, 41, 53

HARNE
  Edieth, 65
  Henry, 65
  Thomas, 65

HARRIS
  Charles, 5, 27, 48
  David, 62
  George F., 109
  Henry, 24
  Honour, 25
  Joseph, 62
  Peter, 6, 25, 56
  Samuel, 7
  William, 111

HARRINGTON
  James, 110

HARTWELL
  John, 110

HAWKINS
  Benjamin, 7, 76
  William, 3, 7

HAY
  Thomas, 78
  William, 7

HAYES, HAYS, HAYSE
  John, 111
  William, 30, 101

HAYNES
  John, 28, 92
  William, 17, 18, 42, 50, 56

HEARD
  Barnet, 35
  Elizabeth, 86
  George, 29, 43, 50, 51
  James, 91
  Jesse, 4, 15, 29, 31, 35, 37, 50, 51, 55, 66, 68, 70, 76, 87, 89, 90, 97, 110
  John, 10, 11, 19, 43, 76, 86, 89, 94
  Margaret, 26
  Stephen, 35, 43, 58, 59, 76, 80, 85, 86, 87, 89, 90, 95, 96, 97, 98, 110, 111
  Susanna, 10
  Thomas, 91, 110
  William, 20, 25, 26, 35, 52, 68, 71, 98
  William, Sr., 25

HELMS
  Benjamin, 94

HELTON
  Jesse, 108
  Solomon, 111

HENDERSON
  John, 7, 54, 110, 111
  Thomas, 7, 54, 109

HENRY
  H., Jr., 39
  Patrick, 58, 69, 79, 87, 94,
    108, 111

HENSLEY
  Benjamin, 110
  Mary, 53

HIBBERT
  Charles, 96, 104

HICKEY
  John, 111

HICKMAN
  Joseph, 105

HICKS
  Benjamin, 12, 97
  Martha, 12
  Miles, 84, 97

HILL
  Robert, 38, 43
  Swinfield, 32, 39, 43
  Thomas, 31, 32, 43, 53, 68,
    74, 101, 111

HILTON, See HELTON

HINTON
  Mary, 27
  William Robert, 26, 27

HOARD, HORD
  John, 80
  Mordecai, 46, 57, 58, 61, 66,
    83, 84
  Sarah, 58
  William, 50, 100

HOBART, See HOLBART
  Harrison, 24, 105

HOBSON
  Mathew, 102

HODGE, HODGES
  Isham, 70, 110
  James
  Joseph, 28, 29
  Josiah, 79
  Peter, 85
  Robert, 106
  William

HODGILL
  James, 9

HOFF, HUFF
  Elizabeth, 86
  Mary, 71
  Samuel, 25
  Thomas, 7, 25, 63, 86

HOLBART, See HALBERT
  Harrison, 89
  William, 10, 106

HOLCOMB
  Juriah, 73, 84
  Grymes, 4, 52, 73, 84, 109

HOLLAND
  John, 92
  Peter, 51, 59

HOLLOWAY
  Barnes, 85
  John, 105

HOLMES, HOLMNS
  Benjamin, 68, 69
  John, 100

HOLT, HOLD
  Ambrose, 72, 76, 77
  Richard, 111

HOOPER
  Ann, 51
  William, 51

HORRELL
  John, 95

HUBBARD
  Benjamin, 52, 73, 102
  Eusibus, 9, 47, 81
  James, 101, 103
  Jesse, 102

HUDSON
  Joshua, 108
  Obediah, 19
  Rhoda, 19
  William Robert, 19

HUDSPETH & CO., 110

HUFF
  John, 83
  Peter, 44
  Samuel, 7

HUGHES
  Archelaus, 3, 5, 7, 19, 32, 37,
    46, 49, 65, 69, 72,
    80, 85, 90, 92, 98,
    99, 102, 104, 107,
    108, 111
  Blackmore, 56, 109

HUGINS
  Luke, 43

HUNTER
  Alexander, 17, 22, 35, 37, 47,
    49, 92, 93, 102
  Charity, 18
  John, 10, 26, 51, 61, 68
  William, 10, 18, 51, 53, 68,
    102, 107

HURD
  John, 24

HURT
  Joseph, 37

HUSK
  John, 23

HUTCHENS
  Frederick, 97

HUTCHERSON
  Philip, 69
  Prudence, 69
  Sarah, 7, 60

HILTON, See also HELTON
  Jesse, 108
  John, 54
  Samuel, 108
  Soloman, 111

INGRAM, INGRUM
  Anthony, 99
  Elizabeth, 56, 57
  James, 82, 90, 98, 100
  John, 56, 57
  Martha, 82, 90, 99, 100
  Pattey, 99

INNES
  Harry, 26
  Hugh, 5, 10, 19, 26, 29, 75, 84
  Mary, 39

IRUS
  Marke, 28

ISAM
  Chart, 86
  William, 107

ISON
  Jonathan, 54
  John, Sr., 109

IVIE
  Howell, 108
  Lot, 16

JACKSON
  Danuel, 59

JAMES
  Jimmy, 82
  John, 82
  William, 68

JAMESON, JAMERSON, JAMISON
  Floreana, 78
  John, 4, 50, 97
  Thomas, 4, 50, 59, 108
  William, 10, 78, 110

JANNEY
  Isaac, 70

JENNINGS
  Miles, 51, 63, 64, 65, 99, 108

JENKINS, JINKINS
  Lewis, 53, 106
  John, 53, 61
  William, 53, 61

JOHNSON, JONSON, JOHNSTON
  James, 84
  John, 7, 62
  Moses, 111
  Samuel, 106, 107
  Thomas, 99

JONNIKIN
  John, 101

JONES
  Abraham, 28, 96
  Ambrose, 8, 28, 36, 39, 51
  Daniel, 79, 110
  David, 14, 44, 47, 101
  Elijah, 13, 47, 55, 70, 83, 96, 101
  Franky, 96
  Harvey, 70
  Henry, 43, 57, 96
  Isaac, 14, 28, 47, 70
  James, 63, 85, 92
  Jeremey, 6
  Jesse, 96
  John, 44, 96
  Joseph, 45, 50, 52, 57, 103
  Mary, 21
  Rachel, 14, 70
  Robert, 2, 44, 47, 70, 73, 96, 99, 111
  Robert, Jr., 13, 14, 27, 62, 63
  Thomas, 6, 21, 45, 47, 50, 52, 57, 70, 71, 92, 103, 111
  Thomas, Capt., 44
  Thomas, Jr., 28, 56, 88, 111
  William, 51, 72, 107
  Winney, 11

JORDON
  Samuel, 37

JOURNICAN, JOURNYKIN
  John, 7, 30

JOYCE
  Alexander, 20, 81, 96, 97

KEATON
  Joseph, 26
  William, 37

KEELE
  John, 109

KEELING
  Alice, 91
  Fanny Alexander, 91
  John Alexander, 91
  Joseph, 91

KEEN
  Carrel, 28, 29
  Elisha, 28
  John, 29, 93, 106
  William, 77

KEETH
　Cornelius, 110

KELLY, KELLEY
　Andrew, 74, 75
　John, 3, 77, 78, 79, 105, 109, 111
　Michael, 85
　Mary, 85
　William, 110, 111
　Winifred, 78

KEMP
　John, 43

KINDRICK
　Elizabeth, 37
　John, 7, 37
　Thomas, 37

KENNON
　Benjamin, 82

KETCHUM
　Elizabeth, 49
　Nathan, Nathaniel, 48, 49

KEY
　Martin, 42, 48, 57, 58, 66

KING
　John, 1, 2, 58, 84, 97
　Joseph, 23, 75
　Walter, 40, 41, 48, 57, 58, 66
　William

KINGTON
　Francis, 77, 79

KINZEY, KINSEY
　Benjamin, 54
　Benjamin, Jr., 54
　David, 102
　James, 102
　John, 55, 88

KIRBY, KEARBY, KERBY
　David, 77
　Francis, 101, 103
　Jesse, 70, 101, 103
　Josiah, 43
　Richard, 74, 107, 109

KISTERSON
　John, 52

KITCHIN
　John, 39

KOGER, COGER
　Henry, 76, 104
　Jacob, 4, 76, 101
　John, 107
　Mary, 76
　Peter, 76

LACKEY
　Adam, 83, 86

LAIN
　Daniel, 92

LAMB
　Walter, 93, 94

LANIER
　D. 81, 97
　David, 4, 12, 54, 59, 84
　Lemuel, 55, 73
　Samuel, 1, 2, 12, 13, 33, 41, 89, 94, 96

LANSFORD
　Henry, 17

LAW
　Henry, 18
　Jesse, 18, 94
　John, 17, 68
　John, Jr., 18
　John, Sr., 68
　Nathaniel, 14, 18

LAWSON
　David, 108
　Norman, 92

LAYNE
　Dutton, 108

LEACHER
　John, 86

LEAKE
　Peter, 93
　Thomas, 18

LEE
　Alexander Brown, 48
　Stephen, 3, 44, 50, 66, 74, 85, 110

LEVINS
　Nicholas Perkins, 10

LEVISTON
　Thomas, 51, 52

LEWIS
　Joseph, 40, 41, 70, 71, 84, 110

LINDSEY
　James, 48
　John, 24, 48

LIVESY
　Thomas, 102

LOCKHART
　Thomas, 88, 100, 107

LOMAX
　Thomas, 40

LONG
　William, 42, 69

LORTON
　Thomas, 50

LOVELL
  Ann Martin, 87
  Daniel, 87
  Martin
  Markam, 87
  Mary Ann, 87
  Robert, 87
  Samuel Moon, 87
  Sarah, 87
  William, 13, 21, 34, 36, 68, 71,
      76, 87, 94

LOWS
  Thomas, 102

LOY
  Stephen, 101, 103

LUMPKINS
  George, 46, 88
  Mary, 46

LUMSDAN
  John, 43

LUTTRELL
  Daniel, 29
  Samuel, 29, 40

LYALL, LYLLS
  Joseph, 29, 106

LYNCH
  William, 74, 108

LYNE
  Edmund, 4, 13, 15, 56, 61
  Henry, 13, 25, 35, 38, 49, 56,
      63, 92
  Samuel, 5

LYON, LYONS
  Elisha, 86
  James, 1, 10, 15, 26, 53, 83,
      84, 105, 106, 108, 109,
      110
  John, 108

LYON & CLOUD, 111

MABRY
  George, 53, 54
  Joseph, 11, 15
  Joshua, 4
  Mary, 4, 15
  Susanna, 11

MACINTREE
  James, 5

MACKINZIE
  Aaron, 16, 26, 100

MADOX
  Hannah, 19
  Michael, 19

MANKIN
  James, 105, 106

MANN
  William, 110

MANNING, MANNUN
  John, 12, 41, 72, 73
  Susannah, 73

MANNON
  Henry, 77

MAOROW
  Jac., 19

MARCUM
  John, 98
  Thomas, 98
  William, 98

MARIS
  Jane (Jean), 20
  Stephen, 20

MARR
  John, 31, 41, 54, 55, 56, 69, 72,
      76, 80, 84, 88, 107, 110,
      111

MARTIN
  Brice, 60, 71, 74, 83, 84, 85
  Charity, 79
  George, 79, 91
  Hugh, 61
  John, 59
  Unity, 85
  William, 71, 82, 90, 99

MARTIN & HORD, 111

MASON
  James, 28, 85, 87
  Robert, 70, 93

MASSEY
  Mordecai, 39

MATHEWS
  Thomas, 82, 100
  Walter, 13

MATLOCK
  Charles, 103
  David, 9, 35, 56
  John, 30
  Margaret, 36
  William, 103, 105

MAVITY
  Mary, 83, 85, 101
  Robert, 44, 85
  William, 13, 14, 43, 44, 47, 55,
      71, 74, 83, 85, 88, 103,
      111

MAYES, MAYSE
  Abraham, 27
  Henry, 27, 46, 81, 101
  Phebe, 27
  Sherod, 30

MAY
  James, 109
  John, 88

MAYBERY
  Joseph, 11

MAYNOR
  Richard T., 111

MAYO
  William, 102

MAXEY
  Sampson, 77, 78, 81

MEAD
  Abirt, 111
  William, 27, 43, 80
  William & Co., 109

MEDKIFF
  Thomas, 110

MEDLOCK
  William, 82

MENESE
  James, 101

MENIFEE
  William, Jr., 21

MELTON
  James, 81

MEREDITH
  Bradley, 103
  James, 40, 41, 74
  Junah, 66

MIEDES
  William, 87

MIERS
  Stephen, 10

MILAN
  John

MILES
  Samuel, 96

MILLER
  Elizabeth, 32, 62
  Haymon
  John Frederick, 4, 6, 31, 32, 61, 107
  Joseph, 105
  Thomas, 3, 32, 44, 62, 110

MINNIS
  Dorothy, 68
  John, 68

MINTER
  John, 15, 33, 46, 47, 49, 50, 81, 87, 100, 111
  Susanah, 87

MITCHELL
  John, 106
  Ralph, 58, 71

MITHIS
  Thomas, 91

MIZE
  Benjamin, 104

MOLLEY
  James, 12

MOOR, MOORE
  Alexander, 32
  Garrott, 108
  William, 27, 32, 81

MOOROW
  James

MORGAN
  Christian, 70
  Haynes, 55, 98
  H., 5
  John, 109
  Lewis, 70
  Mary, 71
  Sarey, 70, 71
  Thomas, 70

MORRIS
  Joseph, 30, 63, 88
  Nimrod, 81
  Samuel C., 44, 45, 88

MORRISON
  Thomas, 74, 107
  William

MORTON
  James, 40, 41
  John, 105
  Lucy, 105

MOSLEY
  Mordecai, 101
  Samuel, 5, 79

MURIS, MIERS
  Stephen, 9

MULLINS, MULLINGS
  Elizabeth, 21
  Jean, 31
  John, 31, 67, 68
  William, 21, 31, 53, 60, 61, 67
  William, Jr., 21

MURCHEL
  John, 6

MURPHY
  Edward, 28
  James, 24, 25, 75
  John, 28, 63, 63

MURRAH, MURROW, MURROUGH
  Jeremiah, 26
  Thomas, 111

MURRELL
  Benjamin, 34, 52
  Jeffrey, 33, 52
  Martha, 52
  Mary, 63
  Richard, 25, 63
  Thomas, 34

MUSGROVE
  B. Estate, 111

MUSICK
  Ellectusous, 107

McBRIDE
  Daniel, 82, 106
  James, 109
  Patrick, 58

McCAIN, McCANN
  Hughey, 27
  Joseph, 66

McCOY, McCOYE
  John, 77
  Richard, 74, 75
  Walter, 111

McCRAW
  Ben, 43
  Jacob, 110

McCRUMP
  William, 102

McDANIEL
  Ann, 9
  Clement, 5
  Isaac, 23, 108, 109
  William, 5, 9, 65
  William, Jr., 5

McDONALD
  Isaac, 53, 54, 95, 96
  Mary, 53, 54

McGHEE
  Holden, 85

McKEEN
  Alexander, 13, 27, 33, 46, 84
  Hugh, 33
  Thomas, 46

MACKENZIE
  Aaron, 16, 26, 38

McKINNER
  Jinnet, 38

McPEAK
  William, 97

McWILLIAMS
  Hugh, 110

NAIL, See NEAL

NANCE
  Ruben, 40, 41, 81, 87

NASH
  Agness, 100
  Arthur, 79
  Marvel, 33, 39, 68, 88, 94, 100, 110

NEAL
  Benjamin, 62, 82, 84
  John, 111

NEVILS
  John, 74, 107, 111
  Sarah, 74

NEWMAN
  Daniel, 80, 104
  John, 80, 93, 104
  Martha, 104

NEWPORT
  Richard, 36

NICHOLAS
  John, 63, 64

NORRIS
  John, 50, 92

NUNN
  Elizabeth, 60
  Thomas, 70, 85

OAKES
  John, 90

O'BRIAN
  John, 109

O'BRYANT
  Dennis, 21

OLDAKERS
  Jacob, 70, 85

OLDHAM
  James, 108
  John, 22

OWENS
  Christopher, 61, 66

PACE
  John, 5, 27, 83

PACKWOOD
  Samuel, 71, 109
  William, 71

PARBERRY
  James, 95

PARKER
  Samuel, 107

PARKS
  Joseph, 87
  William, 80, 87

PARSLEY
  Abraham, 108
  Ann, 67
  Nancy, 67
  Richard, 67
  Thomas, 109

PARR
  Henry, 107, 111
  John, 10, 22, 90
  John, Sr., 37, 108, 109
  Miriam, 22

PATTERSON
  Cecely (Crisly?), 3, 4
  Jarrott, 24
  Samuel, 3, 4, 8, 40, 41, 60, 68,
          70, 79, 85, 91, 104, 110,
          111

PATEN
  Phipses, 34

PATTON
  Benjamin, 17
  Thomas

PAYNE
  Abraham, 57
  John, 18
  Josiah, 18
  Nancy, 77
  Reuben, 18, 32, 54, 57, 59, 77,
          100

PAXTON
  Joseph, 110

PEAK
  John, 58

PEARSON
  Elizabeth, 33
  Joseph, 27, 28, 29, 33

PEDIGO, PEDEGOY, PEDIGOW, PEREGO
  Edward, 3, 6, 109
  Joseph, 67, 79, 100
  Robert, 67, 79, 81, 106, 111

PENN
  Abraham, 1, 3, 15, 18, 21, 22,
           23, 25, 35, 36, 40, 46,
           49, 55, 58, 60, 69, 74,
           75, 93, 96, 101, 102,
           104
  Ruth, 74

PENSEY
  Robert, 111

PERKINS
  Nicholes, 3

PERRYMAN
  Benona, 68
  Daniel, 85, 87, 92
  Jehu, 92
  Richard, 50, 68, 97, 110
  Robert, 50, 80, 111

PEW
  David, 96

PHELPREY
  John, 110

PHILLIPS
  John, 103

PHILPOTT
  John, 24, 106, 111
  Samuel, 106

PIGG
  Charles, 104
  James, 84, 110

PILSON
  Richard, 63, 86

PINKARD
  John, 26, 38, 40, 41

POLLARD
  Francis, 64

POLLY
  Edward, 8

POOR
  George, 109, 110
  William, 90, 107

POSEY
  Humphrey, 5

POTEET
  James, 3, 6, 52

POTTER
  Benjamin, 99
  Lewis, 99
  Thomas, 14, 90

POWELL
  Robert, 8, 56

POWER
  Jack, 37

PRATOR, PRAYTOR
  Miah, 100
  Nehemiah, 107

PRATT
  Jonathan, 46
  John, 46

PREWITT
  David, 30

PRICE
  Charity, 50
  Joseph Shores, 50, 85
  Showers, 66

PRILLAMAN, See also BRILLIMAN
  Daniel, 109
  Jacob, 28, 29, 105, 111

PRIMAN
  Bernard, 92

PREMONS
  Richard, 95

PRUNTY
  James, 98, 106, 111
  Mary, 84
  Robert, 33
  Thomas, 25, 29, 33, 43, 60, 69,
          74, 79, 84, 85, 88, 101,
          104

PULLIAM
  John, 88, 98, 110, 111

PURSELL
  John, 21

PUSEY
  Robert, 71

PYRTLE
  John, 39, 92, 94

RADMUN
  Rhodon, 71

RAGLAND
  Joel, 44, 47

RAILEY
  Phillip, 43

RAINS
  John, 26

RAMSEY
  George, 69, 70
  John, 31, 69, 70
  Mary, 69, 70

RAMY, REAMY
  Daniel, 25, 48, 57
  John, 13

RANDAL
  John, 98

RANDOLPH
  John, 110
  Samuel, 78, 79
  Thomas Mann, 4, 16, 40, 45, 56,
               61, 62, 63, 85, 92,
               92, 99, 101, 102
  Thomas, 49, 63

RANDOLPH, HARMER, KING, 40, 86, 100

RATLIFF
  John, 109
  Silas, 73, 102
  William, 73

RAY, REA
  Andrew, 13, 41, 77, 108
  James, 83
  John, 65, 109
  Thomas, 53, 60

READ
  William Isaac, 5

REDD
  John, 92, 93, 99

REED
  William, 110

REAL, RELL
  Michael, 44, 45

REAMEY, See RAMY

REGAN
  Con, 77

REAVES, See RIVES

RENNO, RENO
  John, 39, 90, 93, 94
  Stephen, 77, 90

RENTFRO
  Ester, 99
  James, 22, 23, 28, 47, 99
  James, Jr., 99
  Jesse, 28
  John, 23, 63, 70, 85, 111
  Joshua, 23, 45, 47, 63, 74
  Isaac, 23, 28
  Mark, 52, 70
  Moses, 2, 22, 28,
  Samuel, 43
  Susanna
  William, 23, 28, 57, 58, 109

RETTER
  John, 74

REYNOLDS, RUNNOLDS
  Bartlett, 107
  Georgesa, 81, 106
  Jesse, 98, 107
  Joseph, 27
  Moses, 107, 111
  Richard, 27, 83, 102, 107

RIAN, See RYAN

RICE
  Daniel, 84, 109
  Henry, 6, 19
  John, 36, 65
  Mary, 36, 69
  William, 77, 79

RICHARD
  Elisha, 72

RICHARDS
  Edward, 43, 73
  Elizabeth, 73
  Shadrick, 73

RICHARDSON
  Amos, 15, 16, 25, 26, 30, 31,
        33, 40, 41, 42, 47, 97,
        98, 99

RICHARDSON, Cont'd.
  Amos, Jr., 25, 30, 31
  Daniel, 16, 26, 38, 40, 41, 104
  John, 30, 73, 93, 94, 96, 97, 108, 109
  Martha, 98
  Thomas, 79

RICKMAN
  Peter, 110, 111

RIGIOR
  Jacob, 75

RITTER
  Abraham, 75

RITTURE
  George, 23

RIVES, REAVES
  Alexander, 54, 61
  Burwell, 61
  Frederick, 14, 15, 28, 33, 38, 54, 60, 61, 90
  George, 73
  Patty, 54

ROBERTS
  Elizabeth, 49
  Joseph, 42, 49
  Thomas, 61

ROBERTSON
  Archibald, 12, 13, 73, 77
  Arthur, 13
  John, 76
  Walter, 98

ROBINSON
  Thomas, 53

ROGERS
  David, 26, 107, 108
  George, 110

ROSS
  Daniel, 32, 74

ROADES, RHODES
  Christian, 5, 9, 16, 35
  Elizabeth, 35

ROWLAND
  Ann, 94, 95
  Baldwin, 23, 59, 60, 71
  Elizabeth, 47
  George, 31, 35, 41, 54, 55, 58, 59, 88, 94, 95
  George, Jr., 88
  John, 1, 6, 15, 16, 23, 31, 49, 54, 60, 74, 94
  John, Sr., 50, 54
  Mary, 23
  Michael, 47, 49, 55, 66, 73, 83, 84, 85, 92, 103

RUBELL
  Owen, 44

RUCKER
  Gideon, 16

RUNNOLDS, See REYNOLDS

RUSSELL
  William, 29

RYAN
  Daniel, 52, 73
  Darby, 13, 14, 23, 27, 43, 44, 57, 70, 73, 74, 76, 83, 84, 88, 111
  Mary, 73
  Obedience, 58, 60
  Philip, 25, 34, 35, 40, 41, 58, 65
  W., 84
  William, 9, 16, 29, 30, 31, 60, 68, 71, 93, 97, 104, 106

SALMON, SOLMON
  Drury, 53, 76
  Hezekiah, 23
  John, 1, 3, 4, 5, 15, 16, 17, 24, 31, 37, 40, 49, 61, 63, 67, 69, 70, 75, 82, 83, 88, 89, 92, 98, 105, 106
  Rowland, 102
  Thadeus

SALSBURY, SOUSBURY
  Jeremiah, 60

SAMMONS
  Elizabeth, 91

SAMS
  John, 42
  William, 77, 106, 108

SANFORD
  George, 81
  John, 81

SANSON, See also SWANSON
  H., 65

SAUNDERS, SANDERS
  Judith, 77
  Mary, 77
  Peter, 1, 4, 21, 27, 32, 70, 74, 77, 90, 103

SCALES
  Nathaniel, 102

SCHNEES
  John, 99

SCOGGINS
  Humphrey, 81

SCRUGGS
  Gross, 99
  James, 93
  Julius, 66

SENTER
  Stephen, 42, 100, 111
  Susannah, 100

SHARD
  James, 108

SHARP
  William, 88, 96, 111

SHAW
  Isias, 96
  Josias, 42, 54, 94

SHEALDS
  John, 75

SHELBY
  Isaac, 39

SHELTON
  Azariah, 109
  Eliphaz, 17, 26, 109, 110
  James, 4, 5, 16, 37, 42, 45, 61, 63, 64, 93
  Jeremiah, 104
  John, 109, 110
  Mary, 27
  Palatiah, 27, 108, 110
  Philiphiah, 16
  Ralph, 3
  Ralph, Jr., 7
  Samuel, 44
  Spencer, 5
  Susanna, 7
  William, 16, 45, 61

SHERIDAN
  Philip, 43

SHOCKLEY
  Chalton, 5
  Levy, 5

SHORT
  James, 54
  John, 58, 86, 87, 98

SIMS, SIMMS
  Bartlett, 109
  Ignatious, 8, 20, 33, 54, 59, 75
  James, estate of, 110
  John, 3, 96, 97, 108
  Sephiah, 3
  William, 30

SIMMONS
  Ann, 83
  John, 20, 72, 77, 78, 83, 90, 96, 106
  Nancy, 20, 90

SKILMON
  Christopher, 71

SMALL
  John, 109

SMITH
  Anthony, 42, 51, 62, 63, 65, 98, 108
  Archibald, 6, 41, 42
  Bird, 47
  Burkes, 99
  Daniel, 107
  Bradley, 63
  Drury, 30, 101
  Edward, 29, 75, 76
  Francis, 81
  Gideon, 111
  Guy, 47
  Henry, 109
  Isaac, 45, 76
  James, 40, 105
  John, 28, 29, 46, 51, 52
  Josiah, 16, 26, 45, 62, 63, 107, 108
  Laddock, Zadock, 111
  Martha, 51, 52
  Munford, 110
  Samuel, 29, 95
  Stephen, 64, 99
  Thomas, 30, 53, 99, 110
  William, 84, 107, 116
  Zachariah, 30
  Zadock, Laddock, 111

SNEED
  John, 73, 102

SOLAMAN
  Drury, 53, 76

SOUTHALL
  Frances, 25
  James Barret, 25

SOUTHERLAND, SUTHERLAND
  Philimon, 43, 48, 63

SPALDIN
  Thomas, 28, 29

SPANGLE, SPANGLER
  Daniel, 34, 105

SPENCER
  James, 24, 45, 59

STALLING
  Jacob, 12, 62, 80

STAMPS
  Timothy, 8, 9, 11

STANDEFER, STANDIFER
  Ismael, 43
  James, 60, 74, 101
  James, Jr., 43, 52, 101
  James, Sr., 43, 44, 101
  Luke, 50
  Israel, 43, 46, 50, 76, 110
  Susannah, 46, 50
  William, 45, 50, 57, 58, 70, 71, 103

STANDLEY, STANLEY
Christopher, 102
William, 10, 50, 51

STAPLES
John, 63, 74
Samuel, 104

STEGALL
William, 17, 61, 97, 98

STEPHENS
John, 108
Stephen
Thomas, 62
William, 42, 52

STEWART
John, 43, 111
Rachel, 11
William, 11, 51

STINNET
Benjamin, 6, 7, 37
Usley, 6

STOCKTON
John, 3
Mary, 71
Robert, 36, 51, 54, 58, 74, 93, 108
Thomas, 4, 71, 109

STOAKES, STOKES
John, 23, 40, 41, 75
Thomas, 17

STONE
Eusebeous, 60, 67, 68
Stephen, 67

STOVER
Jacob, 59

STREET
Joseph, 99
Samuel, 26, 32, 110

STULTS
George, 111

STUMP
Peter, 110

SUMPTER, SUMPTON
Admund, 73
Agge, 73
George, 73, 111
Henry, 37, 71, 73, 82, 89, 108, 110

SWANN
Jonathan, 13

SWANSON, SANSON
H., 65
John, 48, 68
Mary, 63
Nathan, 29, 42, 48
William, 29, 34

SWANSON, Cont'd.
William, Jr., 48, 81
William, Sr., 48, 58, 63

SWEET
Samuel, 6

SWINNEY
Edmond, 104
Edward, 111

TACKETT
William, 13, 81

TALBERT, TALBOT
Isham, 90

TALBOTT & MEAD, 111

TALBORN
Eloner, 12, 78

TALER
Joseph, 99

TARPINE
James, 44

TARRENT, TARRANT
Larken, 105
Leonard, 30, 31
Samuel, 13

TATE
Caleb, 21, 39, 99
Cales
Henry, 108, 110
Robert, 56

TATUM, TAYTOM
Edward, 53, 55, 59, 65, 111
Martha, 65

TAYLOR
Daniel, 13
George, 6, 7, 63, 64
James, 31, 35, 40, 41, 78, 88, 89, 94, 95, 107, 108, 110
William, 53, 76, 108

TERRY
Nathaniel, 9
Thomas, 100
William, 9

THARP
William, 5, 111

THOMAS
Augustine, 65, 102
Benjamin, 94
Charles, 108
Mary, 94, 95
Philip, 2, 40, 41, 94, 95

THOMPSON
James, 39
Joseph, 78

THOMSON
　Lewis, 16
　Mary, 16

THRAILKELD, THRELKELD
　Thomas, 38, 60

THORNTON
　Luke, 59, 108

TINCH
　John, 33

TIRA
　John, 98

TITTLE
　Anthony, 91, 107
　Peter, 91

TOLBORN, TORBORN, TURBORN
　Elonor, (Ellnnioner), I, 38, 94
　Helenner, 78

TOWNSON
　Thomas, 98

TRENT
　Brient, 85
　Henry, 59
　John, 59
　William, 59, 86

TROUPE
　Jacob, 83

TUCK
　Moses, 79

TUNSTALL
　William, 1, 5, 13, 15, 16, 31,
　　　　　33, 38, 46, 54, 66, 67,
　　　　　92, 93, 94

TURNER
　James, 72, 74
　John, 25, 34
　Josiah, 107
　Mary, 38
　Shadrack, 28, 107, 108
　William, 23, 28

UNDERWOOD
　Samuel, 86, 87

VANDEVENTER
　Abraham, 79, 84
　Mary, 79

VARDEMAN
　Peter, 2, 23, 34, 44

VAUGHAN
　Aris, 35, 71
　Henry, 35, 39
　Thomas, 110

VERNON
　Thomas, 86

VESS
　William, 109

VINCENT
　Mary, 47
　William, 43, 47, 98

VINSON
　William, 34

WADE
　Bartlett, 64, 105
　Robert, Jr., 32
　Zaphaniah, 100

WALDEN
　Joseph, 82, 90
　Nathaniel, 90
　Nathan, 82
　Nolan, 82
　Robert, Sr.
　Sarah, 82
　William, Jr., 82, 99

WALKER
　Elisha, 14, 53
　George, 18
　Joel, 62
　Joseph, 9
　Samuel, 62, 63

WALLER
　George, 10, 21, 40, 41, 49, 66,
　　　　　75, 83, 99, 100

WALTON
　Robert, 27, 86, 102

WARREN
　Thomas, 31
　William, 108

WARRING
　Henry, 29

WATKINS
　George, 111

WATSON
　John, 35, 81, 82, 93, 110
　Michael, 6
　Pheebe, 100
　Robert, 67, 79, 107
　Samuel, 67, 83, 100
　David, 36

WATTS
　Thomas, 104

WEAKS, WEEKS
　William, 44, 101

WEATHERSPOON
　William, 110

WEBB
　Elizabeth, 65
　Isham, 110
　Merry, 65
　Sylvanas, 88
　William, 18, 34, 110, 111

WEEKLY
  Robert, 59

WELLS
  John, 40, 41, 49, 50, 75, 87, 88

WEBSTER
  Joseph, 78, 82, 103

WELSH, WELCH
  Richard, 76, 107

WEST
  William, 65

WHITE
  Jesse, 66

WHITSITT
  Elener, 101
  William, 74, 93, 100, 101

WILBURN
  John, 35

WILKS
  John, 48

WILLIAMS, See also GWILLIAMS
  Edgecomb, 10, 74
  James, 33
  John, 58
  R. 70, 98
  Silas, 82

WILLIHAM, WILLINGHAM,
  See also DILLINGHAM
  Fanny, 12, 94, 95
  Frances, 12, 13
  Jesse, 1, 13, 73, 78, 90, 94,
      96, 109
  John, 12, 108
  Joshua, 16
  Mary
  Thomas, Sr., 1, 2, 12, 13
  Thomas, Jr., 2, 12, 13

WILLIS
  David, 17, 57, 79
  Henry, 44, 107
  Isiah, 96
  John, 44, 107
  Thomas, 108

WILLS
  John, 40, 70

WILTON, WITTON
  Richard, 17, 80

WILMOTH
  William, 89

WILSON
  Daniel, 31, 81, 109
  Jesse, 110
  John, 32
  Martha, 80
  Mary, 80
  Richard, 65

WILSON, Cont'd.
  Thomas, 80, 81
  William, 107

WIMBISH
  John, 7, 19, 98, 109

WITCHER
  William, 17

WITT
  Charles, 63
  David, 101
  Jesse, 29, 62, 63, 88, 101
  John, 29, 110

WOMACK
  Abraham, 3

WOOD
  John, 108

WOODING
  Richard, 5

WOODS
  H., 32
  Hugh, 110
  Robert, 1, 22, 59, 61, 62
  William, 62, 89, 100, 110, 111

WOODSON
  Elizabeth, 35
  John, 35
  Obediah, 10, 11
  Shadrick, 66, 74

WOOLVERTON
  Andrew, 90

WYATT
  John, 11, 40

WYNNE
  William, 104

YEALY
  Bainaba, 87

YOUNG
  Allen Ridley, 8, 100
  Archibald, 80, 100
  Edward, 3
  John, 109
  Peter, 14, 70
  Ridley, 80
  William, 42, 57, 58, 80, 81, 99,
      100